Jonathan has survived knives being thrown across the classroom, a pupil jumping out of a window and overseen the confiscation of a Porsche. He has been in leadership positions with failing schools as well as some of the best in the country. Jonathan has taught the children of kings and presidents, along with those from deprived housing estates in the UK in both state and independent sectors. The international school he headed in Canterbury was rated by inspectors as excellent in every area. He finished his career as headteacher of a prestigious British school in central Asia which was rated as having top international practice in seventeen out of nineteen areas.

His schools also have won the Boarding School of the Year Award from the Times Educational Supplement along with awards for excellence and innovation. His school was shortlisted for UK Independent School of the Year, and gained the International Schools Award. Jonathan has won two Global Business Excellence Awards and has been shortlisted for a wide range of other awards. He is also a published writer and was awarded the Order of the British Empire in 2014 for services to education.

Underneath it all, he has championed student voice, working closely with staff and treating others with dignity and respect. Jonathan has risen above false safeguarding allegations, ill health and the challenges of turning around failing schools, and is able to smile and count himself incredibly fortunate to have had a career working with so many amazing people.

For Jackie, Philippa and Alex, and the many great friends who have been with me on my journey—and for Nurdos Khamidullayev and the people of Kazakhstan, who will always have a special place in my heart.

# Jonathan Ullmer

---

# JUMPING OUT OF THE WINDOW

## Courageous Leadership

AUSTIN MACAULEY PUBLISHERS

LONDON · CAMBRIDGE · NEW YORK · SHARJAH

A CIP catalogue record for this title is available from the British Library.

ISBN 9781035856411 (Paperback)
ISBN 9781035856428 (Hardback)
ISBN 9781035856435 (ePub e-book)
ISBN 9781035867080 (Audiobook)

www.austinmacauley.com

First Published 2025
Austin Macauley Publishers Ltd®
1 Canada Square
Canary Wharf
London
E14 5AA

To succeed in any leadership endeavour, you must have networks of strong support around you, particularly when the going gets tough. My immediate and wider family have quite simply been amazing in their unstinting support and care. It was always important for me to make sure my wife and I had weekends away, and our annual two-week holiday with the children was always sacrosanct. They put up with my international travel and strong demands of work amazingly, and to have the support of friends and family is worth more than can possibly be measured. I owe a great deal to my wife, Jackie, and to the persistent support of my children, Philippa and Alex.

Friends have likewise played an ongoing and powerful role over my whole career and their support, care, advice, teasing and support has enabled me to do so much I would never otherwise have thought possible. Some stand out over many years, and David Elcock and Peter Dominey are certainly two of them—from helping me recuperate while I was in Malta, to just 'being there' when I needed them. Steve Capper and Janey Avery have given strong professional support and it has been a pleasure working with them. I am also grateful to David Olde for all the help and support he gave as a senior teacher much earlier in my career.

Georgios Mesazos proved a loyal ongoing friend, and back in Leigh and Westcliff, Tim and Sally Willcock, Nicola and Andrew Palmer and Sharon Ellacott have been brilliant and never failed to keep in touch or check up on me. Tom Loh was a great support and always showed his Christian faith in both help and action. There are so many more—within the Cambridge Education Group's international family along with former students who went out of their way to help. Anslem Waring and Mark Powney were among them, along with so many colleagues from schools over the years.

A particular mention has to go to the admin team—Claire, Liz, Gill, Chris, Lesley, Rebecca and Paula who followed me after I had left their school and frequently visited to check up on me! They were an amazing team. Dawn Pettifer has been unstintingly loyal and supportive through much of my career, as has Kerry Cosson and Rachel Tipple, and I owe thanks to hundreds of others who have stood with me and my family with amazing loyalty and love. To name everyone would take pages, but you know you are all so much appreciated. I have valued contact with all of you and it always brings great pleasure to hear from former students and staff again.

Thank you to all of you, for everything.
Jonathan

# Table of Contents

# Preface

One of my very first lessons in leadership was at Temple Grove School in Sussex, England. At the young age of nineteen, I found myself stepping into the role of their newest teacher. Excited, and eager to make a positive impact, I assigned the class an exercise. Little did I know that this would lead to a rather unexpected turn of events. One student, Matthew, immediately caught my attention when he stood on his chair and boldly proclaimed, "If you make me do that work again, I'm going to jump out of the window." As shock rippled through the classroom, I instinctively told him to sit down immediately. However, much to my astonishment, Matthew turned around and actually jumped out of the window.

Luckily for both Matthew and my budding career, the classroom happened to be on the ground floor, thus averting any severe consequences. Nevertheless, this incident served as an early lesson in educational leadership: simply telling people what to do in a blunt manner often leads to resistance. This encounter left a lasting impact on me, shaping my understanding of effective leadership in the realm of education.

As I embarked on my journey, I quickly discovered that creating outstanding schools wasn't an overly complicated task. In fact, it could be accomplished by teachers and educational leaders who were willing to learn valuable lessons from one another. Whether you were a novice educator, eager to spearhead change, or a seasoned professional with years of experience under your belt, you had the power to make a difference in the lives of young individuals and contribute to the creation of exceptional schools.

My personal journey commenced at the age of nineteen when I began working as an unqualified English and French teacher in a traditional boarding school in East Sussex, England. From there, I pursued further studies at Oxford University and underwent teacher training, including a term of teaching practice at a diverse all-ability school located in the heart of a bustling town. Subsequent to this, I ventured into demanding areas in both Kent and Essex, serving as an English teacher before taking on leadership roles that pushed a failing school towards success.

Armed with the knowledge and experience I gained in school improvement, I transitioned to a leadership position in an independent sixth-form college. However, this move opened my eyes to the fact that independent schools, although grappling with similar challenges as their state counterparts, were far more adept at concealing their shortcomings from the public eye.

My final appointment took me overseas to Kazakhstan, where I assumed the leadership of an international English school catering to students of all ages. Through diligent effort from everyone, we managed to turn around the institution, achieving commendable results during inspections.

My career path took me through the toughest schools until I found myself among some of the best. Regardless of the sector you hail from, I hope you find relatable experiences and insights within the pages of this book. It is important to note that the book draws inspiration from various scenarios both in the UK and overseas, without directly correlating to real individuals or places. We all require guidance and inspiration, learning from the mistakes and triumphs of others, and adapting these lessons to our own work environments. If only I had been fortunate enough to come across a book like this earlier in my career, perhaps I could have avoided many of the challenges I encountered along the way.

Throughout our professional lives, we experience highs and lows. It is through learning from these experiences, adapting, and forging ahead that we can minimise errors and heartache. This book serves as my earnest attempt to offer a real-life perspective on leadership issues within the field of education. Regardless of whether you are a teacher or leader within an educational organisation, the realm of education presents both challenges and tremendous rewards. We must remember that leadership isn't confined to the later stages of our careers; rather, we can embody leadership traits from the very beginning which will prepare us for anything we face in the future. It's how I have been able to weather challenges, false allegations and unpleasantness when they have come, and still emerge with a strong faith and belief in others. Making a difference can certainly be difficult and hard work at times.

To emphasise this point, I'd like to share an old teaching-related poem that my mother once shared with me:

*The teacher stood at the pearly gate,*
*Her face was worn and old.*
*She stood before the man of fate,*
*To gain admission to the fold.*
*"What have you done?" St Peter asked.*
*"To gain admission here?"*
*"I've been a teacher, sir," she said.*
*"For many and many a year."*
*The pearly gate swung open wide,*
*St Peter rang the bell.*
*"Come in," he said, "and choose your harp,*
*You've had your share of hell."*
Anonymous

## Note for Our American Readers

Students in the UK take a series of exams at age sixteen, which are called GCSEs (General Certificate of Secondary Education). They take another series of exams at age eighteen called A-levels (Advanced levels). A-levels are usually taken in three to four subjects and GCSEs in eight to ten subjects. Students at a smaller number of schools and many eighteen-year-old international UK students take the International Baccalaureate (IB) diploma instead of A-levels. For ease of use in this book, I have referred to these exams as "exams taken at age sixteen" or "Advanced-level courses taken at age eighteen." The TRA is the Teachers Regulatory Agency, which can ban teachers on the whim of a panel without concrete evidence. And Ofsted is the government inspections agency in the UK that can issue one word damning summaries of schools in spite of all the excellent things they may be doing.

As you read the stories in this book, I hope you will glean useful information on how to lead effectively in the educational field, whether as a teacher or formal leader. I hope you will be inspired and a bit more equipped to face any challenges ahead.

Jonathan Ullmer

# Chapter 1
# Learning the
# Basics of Leadership

*If you can't take the pressure, you might as well pack your*
*bags and go home…*

I embarked on my teaching career in the late 1970s at
Palmerston School, a private preparatory school in Suffolk.
As one of the oldest—and a top-five prep school in the
nineteenth century—it boasted the famous pilot Douglas
Bader, Foreign Secretary Earl Grey, and second Duke of
Wellington among its "old boys" (former students). It was a
school bursting with life and full of lessons for a young,
unqualified teacher like me. Early experiences are certainly
formative, so it's good to reflect back on how it all started and
the lessons I learned from it all. Developing leadership skills
begins at the outset of one's professional journey, rather than
in the middle or at the end. The lessons we learn early on can
significantly contribute to shaping our future trajectories.
With that in mind, this memoir aims to be a guide as you
navigate the uncharted territory of teaching or embark on a
new leadership role. Our personal stories may differ, but if we
pause and reflect, we can uncover pertinent messages to learn

from. Discovering lessons from the mistakes of others can certainly assist us in avoiding similar pitfalls. As Napoleon reportedly once said, "Fools learn from their own mistakes. I prefer to learn from the mistakes of others." At the end of each chapter, I will offer a concise summary of the key points conveyed, and feel free to contribute your own insights as well.

So, as a young inexperienced novice, I became the new English teacher, as well as being master in charge of rifle shooting and swimming. I also supported the boys working on the extensive grounds of Palmerston School. One day while leading this group from the front, I jumped onto a large log that acted as a gangplank onto an island in the lake there. Gingerly, several boys followed me, clearly uncertain as to whether it was safe.

"Don't be silly!" I cried, jumping up and down on it alongside the young workers who had finally mustered up the courage to join me. At the height of my confidence, the log then broke, throwing all four of us into the muddy water below. I wasn't quite sure at the time what that taught me, but I later realised it had something to do with how people will follow an enthusiastic lead; therefore, as a leader, it's important to know exactly what you are doing!

One of the naughtiest boys I had the pleasure of teaching was Jeremy Hunt—who has now served as Foreign Secretary, managed the UK's finances as Chancellor of the Exchequer, and come a close second to Boris Johnson for the position of Prime Minister. Today, many see him as "safe"—and even perhaps as a less exciting pair of hands than others—but I believe that Jeremy has been clearly underestimated. As a boy, he had a mischievous sense of humour and a sheer determination to do things his way. For that reason, I wasn't surprised in the least to see him earn £14 million from selling his own company, or to watch his exceptional career in politics. This goes to show that the most difficult of young people can often be the most talented. *As a lesson in leadership, one must not confuse obedience and docility with talent or merit.*

For me, teaching at Palmerston School involved working in a bastion of privilege. One of the boarding staff was Princess Diana's flatmate before she married Prince Charles and I once gave one-to-one lessons to the son of a Romanian prince. I was later to be invited to meet his father in their apartment in Paris. But in spite of enjoying these experiences, I knew they didn't represent the real world. Nor did they represent the full scope of experiences I had while working there.

Working in a stunningly beautiful country estate with woods and ponds and many talented and caring staff did not compensate for the tears and crying I used to hear from the dormitories as the pupils began their new terms at what was a traditional boarding school. Then again at the end of the term, I witnessed different emotions. I once felt heartbroken to see a pupil left behind, as his parents had forgotten to pick him up.

This was a different age, as boys were ranked based on all their marks over the term, and class lists began with who had been top of the class the previous term. What this did to those consistently at the bottom of the list really makes me shudder today. Perhaps it instilled a survival of the fittest, but seeing the tears of a mother whose son had only come second instead of his usual first one term simply illuminated the ridiculousness of the situation.

This experience made me think back to days in my own village as a child, where after the iniquitous eleven-plus tests that all pupils then had to take, we would learn our fate for our next steps of education. We would either go to the local grammar school—mine was founded in 1585—or to a school for those who had failed the exam, where we would be forced to leave school early and be judged as failures. After failing my first try at this inadequate exam, I took great pride in later telling young students that I "once failed my eleven-plus but still went to Oxford University." *Setbacks don't have to stifle success unless you let them.*

Fortunately, I had parents who could afford the advantages of private education. They kept me at one such institution, despite having failed this ridiculous test. It just wasn't fair that one test could destroy the life chances of so many, *but in that circumstance lies another lesson about leadership: Life isn't fair. It's just something we must accept, and our job is do our best, maintain our moral integrity, and make a difference wherever we can.*

My mother had been a determined woman and I certainly inherited her character. While her brothers went to top private schools, she argued with her father to let her complete her school certificate and have a career in teaching instead of going into an office before the obligatory marriage. Sadly, when she did marry, she was expected to resign in the 1950s and look after her husband, so she threw her energies into the church and voluntary work with amazing success. When I finally made it to train as a teacher at Oxford and taught at a model all-ability school as part of my course, I took her spirit with me and had quite an experience. As part of my teacher training after I had left Palmerston School and gone to university, I spent one term teaching in a local school, gaining vital, observed experience. Students from there typically either went into farming or local car factory work. I felt challenged to help them see their many alternative options, encouraging them to dream and discover what else excited them.

In the 1980s, I felt that helping students see what the future *could* be and supporting them in their journey to get there was one of the most rewarding and satisfying things I could do for anyone. Many of these young people didn't have rich families or mentors in the right workplaces or jobs. Taking a different path was a struggle for them, but it turned out that many were game to try. In order to help them achieve this success, I would need to win their trust and confidence. Students needed to see that I was invested in them and their future, and that I would be there to support and guide them. Words of encouragement were vital. And systems of brutal competition would need to be replaced with personal challenges and lessons instilling meaning and relevance.

Well, that all sounds good in theory, but as I entered my first lesson with a group of fourteen-year-olds, they ran rings round me. My lack of proper preparation was thrown back in my face. I finally got them quiet and working, but not on work that was meaningful or appropriate. I emerged from the classroom dejected and exhausted.

Instead of a sympathetic ear, my mentor told me, "If you can't take the pressure in the classroom now, you might as well pack your bags and go home…" This statement seemed a tad insensitive, but it certainly challenged me. From that point, I decided to never look back and steadily improve as a teacher in a tough school.

*It is this level of determination in the face of adversity which really makes a difference as to whether you will make a great leader or not.*

As it turned out, some of the lessons I needed to learn were really quite basic.

"Did you realise that in your last lessons, all the questions you asked were to boys?"

I realised that my mentor at Bicester School was spot on. I hadn't seen this one coming, but she was completely right. Having gone to an all-boys' school myself and never taught girls prior to this, I clearly was showing a level of unconscious bias.

This can happen to any of us, making this kind of "hidden curriculum" critical to look out for. *What pupils learn from us isn't always what we think it is.* This is why having other teachers watch us in class can be so important and helpful in ensuring that we truly learn.

Having someone speak freely and honestly to me, challenging my assumptions and practice, was invaluable. It sharpened me and helped me become very open to what and how I was teaching, ensuring that everyone without exception was equally challenged and supported in my classroom. She was the first of many who would mentor me in my teaching career. As a teacher, I also often used fellow head teachers or senior staff to bounce ideas against.

*It's crucial to seek out people with whom you can discuss your practice—what you have enjoyed and what didn't work. Great leaders know how and when to ask for advice. Experiencing a bad lesson can be very disheartening. In cases like this, you certainly need encouragement and someone who will share ideas with you, which you can then try out for yourself.*

The higher you get up the career ladder, the harder it can be to hear good advice, as people may just tell you what you want to hear. After the first assembly I held in a cinema with the entire school present, for example, I was told by a colleague, "Well done Jonathan, I think you presented your points well."

I had to respond honestly, "Well, actually, I thought it was pretty dire. The message on screen was blurred and didn't synch with the sound, and the technical aspects hadn't been rehearsed properly. I should have sorted it a lot better in advance. The pupils were engaged by the novelty of seeing me on a big screen talking to them, but they won't remember the messages."

This story illustrates additional lessons: *From the day you go into teaching, you must get comfortable talking to others and admitting your mistakes while also looking for advice and support. This makes you more human and enables you to learn a lot at any stage of your career.*

As I learned early on about the importance of encouragement and engagement, I often looked for unique ways to pay it forward by supporting young people in their learning journey. One such example came with a bit of acting on my part.

"Where's Mr Ullmer?" a harsh and angry voice exclaimed as a furious, dark-haired woman barged unexpectedly into my classroom. I tried my best to calm her down by lowering my voice, listening, and asking what she was most annoyed about.

"My son was put in after-school detention for eating in class. Well, what would *you* do if you were hungry?"

I explained clearly that her son had actually been chewing gum and sticking it in the hair of someone in front of him before flicking the rest of it at me.

She started to calm down but then suddenly screamed, "Well, I don't care what you think! You assaulted my son by detaining him after school, and I'm going to call the police!"

A siren was heard outside before the "parent" and I started to laugh. We had set the whole scene up as a learning experience. We then asked students to write an account of what had happened in the form of a police statement—to help them with formal and descriptive writing skills. We discussed what kind of words could be used to describe the emotions and events they had witnessed, and then we brainstormed a range of helpful ideas which became their homework to explore in more depth. This also led on to a discussion on anger management during the next lesson. The strong visual dynamics of our scenario inspired some excellent work!

*We must constantly look for new and different ways to engage young people and learn tips and ideas from our colleagues and others. You can't do everything on your own and keep a meaningful work/life balance. You must take shortcuts, integrating other ideas and lesson plans with your own so you don't have to invent everything. Brilliant lesson plans and resources of all kinds reside on the internet, so plunder them, adapt as necessary, and apply them to your situation.*

As I learned to teach, I found other opportunities to help students engage in learning more effectively. In one case, in order to instil the classics, I took on the role of Theseus with a number of others in Milton's *Paradise Lost*, performing a modern and lively enactment which had been written by another friend. After approaching schools in advance to ask permission to present to their students, we toured the production around to other schools helping to bring the voice of Milton alive for many Advanced-level students in the area. As I grew in confidence, I also realised I could get students to perform parts in the touring shows rather than me, which created an incredible learning experience.

I also learned that there's nothing that annoys school leaders more than having things thrust on them at the last minute or when they discover proper planning hasn't been done. It's not the most exciting thing in the world to write out risk assessments, prepare work for others to supervise your classes, or fill out other forms. But this administrative work is still a key part of being a strong educational leader or teacher.

*If you want to keep people on board with you, make sure you do the planning and the boring bits.*

To my shame, it's something I often slipped up on, and it caused myself and others a lot of unnecessary stress.

In a similar vein, I got a group of fifteen-year-olds to re-enact Shakespeare's *Macbeth* in wheelchairs to not only appreciate the world of those without the same movement skills as them, but also to add a zest and urgency to the performance as they discovered the power of movement on stage, sometimes at speed.

"Whatever do you think you're doing?" asked an exasperated deputy head as she heard Shakespearean words being shouted from wheelchairs in the school hall and reverberating around the school. She was more used to teaching that took place at desks in a classroom.

"I'm making Shakespeare come alive," I replied somewhat sheepishly.

"Well did you book the school hall this afternoon?" she fired back at me. Fortunately, on this occasion, I had covered my bases properly and booked the hall we were performing in, and she promptly retreated to her office.

My teacher training finally came to an end, and I prepared for the next steps in my journey into education. Having learned a lot, I was keen to put it all into practice.

Looking back on this experience today, what strikes me most is how these basic lessons in the classroom were so incredibly important in forming a grounding in leadership for me for the future. *A teacher is responsible for a class and accountable to both parents and the school, and thereby gets to use an impressive array of leadership skills. Becoming a good educational leader is about harnessing these basic skills and staying true to them, as the situations you find yourself in will change so much over the years. Times will change, but the basics of leadership don't.*

## Basic leadership rules for education

I learned a lot from the early teaching experiences shared in this chapter, so I would like to sum up with the following key rules to remember.

- **Lead by example**. It's no good telling other people to do things that you clearly won't do. This doesn't mean that you must do other people's jobs for them, but it does mean you should show a willingness to help. For example, if I asked pupils to pick up litter, I made sure they saw me doing it first.

- **Enthuse and inspire others**. People must want to be led, and they need to see your determination and enthusiasm. Once they catch this sense of excitement, they will go with you and buy into what you're teaching.

- **Do the boring bits!** These things are often actually important, and by arranging people to supervise classes when you aren't there, completing visit forms properly, and complying with school regulations, you will create a good impression and avoid a lot of hassle for everyone—including yourself.

- **See the potential in everyone**. Everyone all around us has the potential to do better. As teachers and educational leaders who want to help students, we must look at what makes them excited or what they want to do, and work our plans around this. Don't write anyone off; they could be the foreign secretary or chancellor of the future…

By following these basic leadership rules, we can create an environment that fosters growth, inspires others and ultimately leads to better educational outcomes.

# Chapter 2
# Learning the Hard Way

*She threw a knife at me across the classroom…*

When I first started studying at Oxford, I resolved to do two things my friends would never in a million years imagine me doing: take up rowing and join the army.

Training in the Royal Signals started immediately after school, so I had to get ready and change my clothes before leaving the university campus. I will never forget the expression on the face of my somewhat trendy mentor at the school as I walked in uniform down the corridor towards her. I don't think she ever recovered from the shock of discovering I wore a uniform and was in the army. It certainly shattered her preconceived image of me.

The time comes for most of us when we must get a full-time job and earn money. And in teaching, every new job can be like going back to the beginning. Students don't know you. You haven't yet built up the respect and teamwork you will need with staff and students, which often equates to a tough first few months.

After serving in the army for the Royal Signals while part of Oxford University Officer Training Corps, I started looking at the Royal Army Educational Corps. I was driven to a base for my interview in a dark car. Travelling through the countryside amidst trees and empty fields, it felt like something out of a James Bond film. I was then treated as important while I faced probing questions.

My experience in the training corps had taught me a lot about leadership, as I got to run all over Salisbury Plain, signalling others and working as a team to achieve a goal. I certainly enjoyed shooting guns, watching the backs of others, and using my initiative; but sadly, the army life ultimately wasn't for me. While a great experience, I was also conscious that I was probably bordering on being a pacifist. That mentality didn't really seem compatible with army life…so my pursuit of a military career ended.

So, where next? Well, I spotted this job in a beautiful public school near Bristol, and I applied for the position.

"Welcome to St Saviours," the head teacher said as he guided me through period corridors and well-kept classrooms. A fountain was flowing in the distance, as I was warmly greeted by the department team. The English curriculum I would teach from was a dream, with major writers covered in detail and a supportive team behind the program. I was well-qualified, having worked in a private school and done my teacher training at Oxford. Beautiful flowers bloomed, all the staff seemed serious and academic, and the serene and purposeful atmosphere was beguiling.

But something just didn't feel right. I was being offered the chance of an amazing job, but I slowly came to realise that *being a leader isn't always about going for the easy option.*

My next interview was by telephone with a struggling school in Kent. Its catchment area was a difficult one, and the job would clearly be hard work. The headteacher spoke

31

passionately about the school, mentioning how it was an ideal place to start a successful career. It was clear to me that they really needed people who were enthusiastic and determined to help in challenging circumstances.

"If you can work here, you'll be well placed to teach almost anywhere," he told me.

And he was right. It was a place where equality, openness and integrity mattered, as did giving young people from deprived backgrounds the very best starts in life.

A day later, I had an interview in person at Kingsford School in Kent. It was in an area full of re-settled travellers and people from the East End; many living there didn't seem to have experience with the world beyond the local supermarket.

The moment I arrived on campus, I realised that the independent school in Bristol didn't stand a chance of luring me. I had already started to learn some key leadership lessons, and they led me firmly in the direction of Kent. The headteacher offered to let me set up a drama department while teaching English to their Advanced-level students. As it was August and they hadn't made an appointment, they clearly bent over backwards to meet my teaching preferences.

I knew the position would be a challenge, but I was beginning to learn something: *Leadership itself is a tough challenge, and if you're going to be good at it, you sometimes must throw yourself in headfirst. And there are people out there who need you more than others do.*

After accepting the position in Kent, I moved and managed to get a room in a vicarage attached to a local church in a village nearby. I was ready to start my position!

Rent was cheap, and as I worked, I managed to save to buy my first car. But when I promptly lent it to a friend to practice his driving, he filled it up with diesel instead of petrol fuel. While that nearly destroyed the engine and wiped out my savings till the end of the year, I never had the heart to tell him.

One of life's lessons—incredibly relevant to leadership and which I learned through this experience—is that *we are here to give and not to take, and where there is clear need around us, we may be called to rise to the challenges it poses.* Whether loaning a car, lending an ear, or providing a lesson, I wanted to be a vessel to help others.

Despite my best intentions, I quickly learned that the school was rowdy, filled with young people who knew how to speak their minds. The honesty of their approach was refreshing in some ways, while downright rude in others.

I also learned that teaching these students would be hard work. I did all the right things—lining them up in silence before entering the classroom and teaching them effective, strong lessons. But my time was hardly uneventful.

In one lesson, I suddenly heard a thud beside me on the blackboard. Not thinking much of it, and not realising what she had thrown, I turned around and saw the girl clearly responsible. I gave her a stern look and said, "I'll see you after class when we can talk about this," and then just continued teaching. The class seemed subdued by my calm approach and appeared to work and focus at an even higher rate.

At the end of the lesson, the girl ran straight out and confessed to her head of year: "I threw a knife across the classroom at Mr Ullmer. I don't know why; I just had it in my hand and decided to do it. It only just missed him. But he just looked at me and then went on teaching. He's going to kill me after the lesson."

Well, of course I never killed her, and although it was a daft thing of this student to do, her head of year was well able to handle it. I don't know what my reaction would have been if I had known this was about to happen, but keeping cool in a serious situation paid dividends. The class was more than impressed that learning had continued, and it showed them that nothing they did was likely to shock or throw me.

I certainly wouldn't wish anyone to be in this situation, but there is certainly a clear message for leaders: *keep your cool in spite of whatever happens, and you'll be surprised how it can bring trust and respect.*

But I can't end this story without being completely honest and realistic. I would come to learn that *after major success often come setbacks.*

A few weeks later, I was teaching using a video camera. It was fun, and the students were making short films and improving speaking and listening skills. But when I left the room for less than a minute to get something from the stock room, a boy turned round and dropped his trousers in front of the camera. It was only later that I spotted the footage and promptly deleted it. Horrified with no idea what to do, I alerted my head of department.

It turned out that he was a wise head on older shoulders who advised me: "Jonathan, I know you've deleted it, but pretend you haven't. Then tell the boy you're going to show it to his parents."

What followed was an incredibly uncomfortable interview for the boy concerned.

"James," I started, "give me one good reason why I shouldn't phone your parents at once and ask them to come in to see me and view what you put on this video." He squirmed uncomfortably. "At the same time, I think it would be a good idea if I asked the headteacher to come in and see it as well." He went bright red with embarrassment and I could see the fear and horror in his eyes. I didn't need to do anything more and rest assured, he never caused any trouble again whatsoever.

It was about this time that one of the strict deputy heads who saw the work I did to keep order in the classroom suggested that I observe the other deputy head, Mr Boxforth, while teaching English. This deputy was feared and determined, and never one to cross swords with. I looked forward to watching him in action, with some uncertainty as to what I was going to see.

His class was a bottom set, with some of the most disruptive and difficult students in the school. But as I watched him, I was amazed by how he was clear on his expectations. Yet he also always listened to the students, backed down when he needed to, and kept their respect and a sense of hard work in his classroom.

This teacher allowed me to witness how to be flexible in dealing with people. I learned: *Nothing needs to be completely dogmatic. You can get your way with a wide variety of approaches, and you can switch until you find the right one.*

This was a key lesson for me in effectively leading a group. I learned that this sense of listening and discovering was the best way to lead people forward and keep them *on side*, while knowing which expectations to insist on firmly and which to leave for another day. I was grateful to watch this outstanding teacher in action.

I would have more lessons to learn. The early 1980s represented a time of major union disruption in schools in the UK, and as a teacher in this community, I had to respect the needs of my colleagues as well as those of the students. I became the union rep for one of the main moderate unions which had a policy of not taking any strike action. I had to tread carefully with colleagues who were going on strike, making clear that I respected their position, even though I did not wish to strike myself. There were long rolling strikes and a ban on after-school work. I met with other colleagues in my union, passing on messages and keeping them informed. I was also able to support staff as they went through difficult times on occasion. The position I was put in could easily clash with my responsibilities to the students, as I was also in the middle of running a major after-school musical production which had to be postponed.

As a new teacher in charge of drama, I had work to do to prepare the drama studio, and no official time to do it. I also didn't want to cause unnecessary offence to others by working after school at a time of heightened industrial tension. The caretaker would have been horrified if he knew, but I left a window slightly open at the end of school, then came back late in the evening on my own to paint the new drama studio (an old classroom) black and set up a fully-functioning drama department. Doing this satisfied my desire not to undermine my colleagues, as none of them knew about it. But it also gave the students a running start at building their drama skills and finding a strong voice for themselves.

The class itself came with many lessons and experiences in leadership. In preparation for one of our shows, I borrowed an old coffin from a friend in amateur dramatics and carried it through the window of the drama studio at night. Fortunately, I was not seen, and no questions were asked…

*Good leadership respects and takes account of the views of others, whether or not you agree with them, but it never stops your forward progress. It's self-defeating to annoy or upset people you work with, as you never know when you might need their support.*

The head teacher at Kingsford was a former drama teacher and always a strong support. He taught a couple of lessons of drama per week, and we had occasional department meetings with him over a glass of sherry in his office. Civilisation can survive in all circumstances, and he was a beacon of civility in a harsh world. He gave me opportunities to develop my skills and helped me to fly as a teacher. For example, I had freedom over my curriculum and how to do things, and soon became chair of the West Kent Drama Association. We ran events and productions for parents and students, uniting primary and secondary pupils performing together, which showed the incredible learning experiences to be had on all sides while working so collaboratively. In fact, when one of my tough secondary students quaked with fear at the thought of performing in a pantomime for younger pupils the next day, it was incredible to see the care and sensitivity this student then went on to display in encouraging the younger pupils, discovering parts of himself hidden for many years. Examples like this are why many of us go into teaching. Another production based on the story of Nicholas Nickleby was equally memorable for quite different reasons. "Can you help me marshal this orderly line?" I asked a friend as the production reached a climax. I stood by the hall door as the pupils entered silently holding candles and created a moving effect as they moved through the audience. "I must make my hair look its best on stage," one of the lead actors commented as they were about to move into the hall, and sprayed additional hairspray onto her hair.

You can imagine what happened next as they lined up to enter. The candle caught the hairspray and it suddenly flared up. It was only incredibly prompt action by a teacher that stopped it going any further and not even the girl concerned realised it had happened...! In spite of this, the show was a great success and pupils grew steadily in confidence and maturity. I have been incredibly meticulous about health and safety issues ever since.

As I continued in my role, I realised increasingly that *excellent leadership is about giving people the opportunities to fly—to create things they own and share them with others. It's also about giving people responsibility and supporting them in it.* I was incredibly fortunate in my early teaching years to be given this responsibility and opportunity to fly, and it stayed with me throughout my career.

The head teacher was, if I remember correctly, a member of Rotary, and through it knew another head teacher who worked in a school at Hawksley for children with behaviour and learning difficulties. As we were refraining from after-school activities due to the teachers' industrial actions, he mentioned that this state boarding school was looking for staff to do paid evening and weekend extraneous duties. I had never worked in a school like this, which housed students who came from a range of backgrounds, including some who clearly had been badly neglected. This seemed a million miles from the privileged world of Palmerston School, so I decided to jump in head first again, and off I went to see for myself what the school was like.

Set in wide-open grounds, the school was also situated in Kent, "the garden of England," which was quite a community. I soon made friends with the senior master, who showed me the ropes and let me observe him working with the boys and girls at the school. He again had a style which commanded respect from the students, and he often gave them responsibilities. For example, they would be given his keys to fetch things and were put in charge of a range of activities. He spoke to them as if they were young adults, and they often responded in kind. He always knew how to bring humour into and diffuse a situation. I remember once when one child, in a fit of rage, told him to, "f**k off." Calmly and collectedly, He turned round to her with his inimitable northern accent and told her, "If you're going to use language like that, then at least say it properly." He then repeated the offending word with his own northern accent and its different vowel sound in the middle. She went off, completely deflated and lost for words.

I was astonished at some of the deprived and disruptive backgrounds some of them had come from, yet they were often so incredibly friendly and mature. They clearly appreciated the structure and support they had at the school. The school had its fair share of incidents—these were often young people that mainstream schools had been unable to cope with—but there were considerable successes too. I certainly noted how giving responsibility allowed the most difficult of students to grow.

There was of course always a risk I could fall flat on my face there, but the rewards were considerable also. The senior master was unafraid to take risks and trust people, and he thereby became another leader who made a considerable impact on my own journey towards becoming an effective leader.

I enjoyed leading after-school drama sessions there, working with the young people on their homework or projects, taking them to places with other staff, and giving them experiences they may never have had at home.

Many of the leadership skills I have alluded to in this chapter may seem to come as second nature to you. Still, it never ceases to surprise me how many people haven't realised how important the simplest lessons are, or they haven't demonstrated them in their own work. Although I was a teacher, these leadership skills have clear relevance across many careers and workplaces. Forgive me for restating what many may feel is obvious, but following are some of the lessons I learned during this period of my life.

## More Basic Leadership Lessons

- **Give others responsibility and respect their ideas**. Doing so makes them feel valued and trusted while challenging them to reach new levels of ownership. Those who don't trust others will find it very hard to achieve things on their own. To that end, make time for other people, listen to them, respect them, and work out what makes them tick. Then support and help them. And remember, this applies to students as well as staff.

- **Never be afraid to take risks**. It's easy to play it safe—never sticking your head above the parapet, never challenging. That way, you won't get hurt or tripped up. But you also won't achieve great things. Great results come from pushing boundaries and trying something new.

- **Don't be distracted by side issues**. Your job may be hard enough with all its challenges.

- **Don't annoy others and cause friction**. Instead, make sure your colleagues are treated properly and with respect in everything you do, so you minimise the chances of using up emotional energy with disagreements. Focus on what you are there for, and do it well.

- **Put yourself somewhere where failure is seen as a sign of growth**. Some schools or institutions simply don't value ideas and progress, and they are tightly controlled from above. This is not an atmosphere you will flourish in, so try to find somewhere else to work.

- **Be incredibly flexible.** Things can come at you from all angles. New government regulations, changes in school structures, and exam board changes are all a constant. Just accept this ongoing flux, take it in your stride, and explore ways to manage new things. When I was a head teacher, I remember one worn-out teacher saying to me, "Jonathan, when are things actually going to stop changing?" I had to sympathise but also tell her that sadly, they never would. Society and education are in a constant process of change, and we must accept and get used to it.

# Chapter 3
# Becoming a Leader

*A condom filled with stage blood…*

Meanwhile, in the UK, the national picture in education was moving fast. We were firmly in the 1980s, and UK Education Secretary Kenneth Baker was introducing the National Curriculum, bringing wholescale changes. The teaching of English was changing fast, and along with many other teachers, I can't say I particularly cared for it. New structures were emerging, and the freedom we had enjoyed in teaching was slowly being stripped away. The direction was moving in favour of more accountability and standardisation. The old examinations which had given incredible freedom in many ways were replaced by new ones, and change was very much at the forefront of everything we had to do.

During this time there was a brief period where the arts were allowed to flourish. It looked like taking a visual or performing arts subject could become a compulsory part of the curriculum for fourteen- to sixteen-year-olds. New posts started sprouting in schools for positions like "Expressive Arts Coordinators." Although I had been trained as an English teacher, I could see the freedom in teaching through drama and the arts, contrasted to the constraints that were beginning to envelop English teaching in the UK. As a result of such changes, I decided to apply for some of these roles.

My experience in using drama as an English teacher came to the forefront. I had many press cuttings of exciting initiatives I had been involved in, from letter writing partnerships with Chinese schools to employing the latest technology in school productions. A strong track record of school shows, an innovative approach to teaching, and my rapid promotions at Kingsford soon led to me being offered an interview at Southport Comprehensive School in Southend.

Travelling to Southend was really like moving backwards into a time warp. The old selective grammar schools still dominated the scene, and Southend was one of the few areas left in the UK that still selected students to go to these special grammar schools at the age of eleven. It was a ridiculous system, with children being branded as failures before they began to have a start in life. Educational research had already shown how damaging this could be to young people. Of course, these selective schools had excellent results, which were claimed as a justification for keeping their processes in existence. But these results came at the expense of the lives of too many young people.

Southport Comprehensive School was, however, unusual. It was an all-ability school in the middle of an area which separated students to go to different schools based on their ability. Although open to all abilities, there were disproportionately fewer top academic students at the school. They had instead chosen to go to the local grammar schools.

The Southport School catchment area also included one of the five most deprived electoral wards in the UK. The school was a popular choice for those in neighbouring Leigh and Westcliff whose children had narrowly failed to get into grammar schools. Children were also clearly removed from selective schools on behaviour grounds, and if they failed to conform, they were left to other schools in the area, like Southport School, to pick up.

At least it did have a small number of selective places in a "top stream," so it wasn't a completely non-selective school. It also attracted a few parents who, on principle, didn't agree with the proliferation of grammar schools which Southend on Sea boasted of.

## The interview

My interview was rigorous, but I clearly shone against the more local and traditional candidates with narrower experience of the developing arts scene in schools. I was, at that time, taking a diploma course in the arts and having great fun expanding my experience in dance, art, and music. I had also written in the press about arts projects I had been involved with and promoted the inclusion of different cultures in exploring the arts. Having directed many performances, my technical knowledge showed through in the area of drama.

"So, what would be the first thing you'd do if you were appointed to the school?" someone on the interview panel asked.

"Well, the first thing would probably be to make the school conform to the Health and Safety at Work Act," I replied, listing a wide range of failures in compliance I had seen with regard to the drama and production equipment we had been shown as candidates…

I liked the honesty of the headteacher, Rob Haylo, who was also on the panel and quite upfront that "I've got as much culture in me as that spider plant." He then added, "But I know the value of drama to young people, and I want to see it flourish." I can even remember his exact words. He was quite clear that he had seen the transformational power of drama and the arts in schools, and he knew how powerful they could be for young people.

Here was a man I could clearly do business with, and I accepted the post.

## Imposter syndrome

So, suddenly, I found myself thrown into a leadership position in the visual art, music and drama departments. The head of drama resigned soon afterwards, and the head of art was approaching retirement. I was terrified to start the new job, particularly as my degree had been in English and not drama. I was clearly on my own, without the safety of a big department to support me.

In retrospect, I realise that I suffered from "imposter syndrome," and I'm sure I'm not alone in experiencing this. I had run big shows and was a good administrator, but somehow it never felt like enough. I now had a team of differing subject specialists, and a part of me doubted my skills and ability to lead this effort. Yet change was clearly on the cards.

I realised I needed to move carefully and tactfully. I knew that if I didn't show confidence, I couldn't expect others to follow. I just had to grit my teeth and get on with it.

A lot of my next steps would be all about respecting my new team while not letting anything stop the changes which needed to be made. My new staff were clearly very wary of me, but because I listened to and respected them, the whole process seemed to go so much easier than I had expected. With a supportive head teacher behind me, progress started to be made.

## Working all hours and jumping ahead

One of the first tasks was to start working on a full-scale production. This was no mean feat, as the lighting system sparked when it was used, there were no safety chains, and the sound system was antiquated. But with strong support from the head to claim education authority funding, and the parents' association keen to help out, thousands of pounds were spent on new systems and updating the hall facilities to make it happen. We tackled the endless obstacles—such as the education authority telling me that the school with a special licence to do public performance work was one of the grammar schools, so they didn't need to support me—but I realised *the determination to move forward is a hallmark of good leadership*. I drafted arguments, made funding bids, and was relentless in ensuring we could launch our first show, which was a modern workshop performance of *Oh What a Lovely War*.

The next thing to handle was getting performance work off the ground with staff and pupils. By now, I had recruited an excellent dance teacher, who was certainly game to help, and the head of music and second in the art department threw their lot in with it too.

But a senior teacher at the school stood back and told me unequivocally, "You're just wasting your time. No student has ever turned up for after-school work except for sport. I'd give it up if I were you."

A group of three teachers stood out in this process, and not always in a good way. They were experienced, cynical, and quick to comment on what they thought. Known as the "three witches," they always sat together in the staff room. It didn't take me long to realise they didn't like the new head. Anything he did started them off again, as they cackled about any changes and how things were "so much better before he arrived." It was difficult to stop myself from feeling really low.

Fortunately, however, I had already started building friendships with others outside the school who were an incredible support. As low as I got, they just kept encouraging me. In seeing the difficulties that others also felt, I could better put it all into perspective. I braved the criticism and snide comments and launched rehearsals.

Still, there were enormous difficulties. There was a "late bus" which left to take students home after they had completed detentions for bad behaviour or lack of homework, but even this didn't work for us in getting students home. We needed rehearsal slots of up to two hours to make this work, so the only option was for me to take pupils home in my own car after we had finished. This was allowed by the school to help pupils who lived in Leigh or Westcliff, provided my car had business insurance. Even though it was early safeguarding days, I was careful to always drop off any girls before the boys, and the last pupils to be dropped off were usually those whose parents I knew—often through the parent's association or elsewhere.

I couldn't know this would come back and bite me many years later, but for the time being, I ploughed on with a great team around me.

Suddenly, pupils heard about the production of *Oh What a Lovely War*, and against all the staff's predictions and cynicism, these students started to audition and wanted to take part. We soon had a great, though untested, cast.

I needed to work out which recruits would stay the course throughout and which others showed promise. I wasn't likely to get some of them at all rehearsals, so those could fill small but essential cameo roles.

Senior students and those of all ages were keen to join in, with some helping with sound and lighting till the early hours of the morning! I tried hard to fit in everyone.

### Pushing the boundaries

At this stage, I had an incredibly understanding caretaker. The immense work needed to bring things up to scratch and put on a complex production demanded hours in evenings and weekends to pull it all off! I got in touch with the same friend who had lent me the coffin in Kingsford, and he came up with the original, enormous, mercury rolling news panel which had been used at the first production of the show in Geneva. It was amazing, and having key facts about the war running as a newsreel on the stage made the audience sit up and take notice. We were able to include many incredibly moving scenes by alternating the farcical with harsh facts and death, which I really hoped would move the emotions of the audience.

There were certainly moments when I despaired of it all coming together, as boys started fights while waiting for their scenes and others were sporadic in attendance. Yet as it moved forward and students saw how powerful it was all going to be, their commitment steadily increased. In terms of learning more about leadership, it just re-enforced the importance of *respecting others—including students, not taking no for an answer, and refusing to let events stop you from moving forward.*

There were some incredible moments to look back on…such as was the time when several staff reported me to their union for making a noise in the school hall, which was adjacent to the staff room. They claimed that the drama disturbed their "right for a peaceful lunchtime." Another time, I was suddenly accosted by a member of staff: "Jonathan, whatever are these students doing, adjusting lights at the top of your scaffolding tower? It's dangerous and clearly against the law."

I calmly replied, "Well, I'm conforming with all safety regulations, and this is a usual practice in many schools with strong drama departments—just clearly not at Southport School."

The teacher retreated, horrified, to the staff room.

From my side, we had adhered to all health and safety assessments, but the sight of hundreds of students happily working after school hours—including manning expensive sound and lighting equipment and fixing lights on the ceiling—was just too much for some to take. It took several years for this kind of activity to finally be seen as more "normal" at the school!

This was all pretty nerve-racking! *What if the show doesn't work, the pupils don't turn up, and I've spent thousands of pounds I won't get back?* I thought during my many sleepless nights.

The challenge of realism in the scenes was one I took incredibly seriously. We spent many hundreds of pounds on pyrotechnics, which shocked both students and audiences alike. A favourite scene was one in which fourteen- and fifteen-year-old students, wearing ridiculous army hats, acted out dancing round on imaginary horses…before being gunned down like lambs to the slaughter. To add to the impact, they all made sheep noises as they were gunned down. This represented a fast shift from the ridiculous to the horrific. To enhance this even more, two soldiers were left standing. They were then both shot by single gunshot wounds as blood poured out. These effects were by no means easy to achieve.

To achieve these effects, I worked with an older student who was full of ideas and great at latex modelling. This stage effect involved a condom being filled with stage blood and then getting stuck to the student's chest. A detonator was placed inside the condom, with wires leading from it down the student's arm to a trip switch in his hand. The condom had a metal place behind it to protect him from harm, and his shirt was slightly serrated to tear easily without it being noticed beforehand. As the surviving solders stood in silence among the dead, one after the other flicked their trip switches. Their shirts then ripped open with a gunfire-like shot—with blood pouring forth from the ripped condoms. This horrific scene shocked the audience even more. This was at a time before school violence became a trend, but at the time it was a good example of creative leadership.

The scene ended with a beautiful song sung by one of the older girls as she walked her way through the fallen bodies. This song was meant to encapsulate exactly what the play was trying to say about warfare, and the audience would be stunned into silence. But unfortunately for her, she had not attended rehearsal that day, and she didn't know what would happen next. I delighted in seeing her suddenly cry out, "Oh, sh…" as at the climax to the scene, a further pyrotechnic exploded on the edge of the stage where she was not expecting it. Another key lesson, for her: *be properly prepared!*

Unfortunately for one of the boys, in spite of all our safety preparations, we missed the fact that he had not been properly insulated behind the metal plate on his chest. After the show, he showed us the small red mark it had made. He was fine and laughing about it, but we realised we had to phone his parents and let them know. The dance teacher and I spent some moments trying to work out what to say to avoid any alarm for the poor parents, while also being honest about what had happened. We came up with the expression of saying he had a small "heat mark" on his chest. And we promptly made sure it could never happen again.

But instead of telling his mother more about it when he got home after the call had been placed, the student simply arrived at the front door of his house with the fake blood over his shirt, dropped his trousers, and told his mother, "Look, Mum, my balls have exploded!" …

## The show must go on

Bearing in mind the catchment area of the school, I resolutely steered away from popular shows, instead prioritising productions like this that would stimulate and challenge while helping young people grow in knowledge of history and the classics as a key part of the fun they were having.

During *Oh What a Lovely War*, I managed to persuade the Royal Shakespeare Company to come and do some technical work with the students on the show. And for our next production of *Animal Farm*, the Royal National Theatre came to run workshops that helped pupils grapple with the key themes of the show.

The lessons in these experiences became clear to me: *In whatever we do as leaders, it's so important to involve others—including people at the very top of our field—to help nourish and grow the talent we have. None of us on our own can do everything, and calling in others to work alongside us can add depth and knowledge to our projects. Weak leaders view asking for help as a threat; strong leaders welcome additional input and support, knowing that everyone involved will clearly benefit from it.*

Finally, the day of the show arrived. The three witches had been grinning at me in the staffroom, thinking the event just wouldn't happen. Then with bangs and a flash, the show started—with everyone giving a stunning performance. The production brought tears to my eyes. It felt like a nightmare launching and setting it all up, but the final show got rave reviews and clarified that the arts were there to stay.

*Animal Farm* turned out to be another amazing show. The music was almost un-singable, and I was delighted to see students really have a go at it and manage to pull it off!

Once again, it certainly wasn't easy. It just went to show that *when you throw people a challenge, you will be surprised how often they will rise to it and achieve amazing things!*

You will not be surprised to know that my love of pyrotechnics was still as strong as ever, and we involved them in this show as well. I delegated the explosives box to a great member of staff, and the students involved were also very trustworthy. However, the local newspaper headlines not long afterwards screamed at me: "Student hurt by explosives from science department."

"What on earth did you do?" I asked one of the boys in charge, as I had recognised at once that the science department was probably completely innocent.

"Well, I took two of the pyrotechnics out when the teacher wasn't looking, took them home, and took them apart. Then I put a match to them…"

"Well, I don't regret trusting you," I replied. "But I can't do it again. This has literally blown up in both our faces…It was an incredibly stupid thing to do."

After disciplining the lad, I had to confess all of this to the head teacher—and the local newspaper. This is how the arts department ended up on the front page the next day as the place the explosives had actually come from. It was not the only time I would end up on the front page of a newspaper.

I'd been let down and made to look stupid, so I tightened up all procedures. Then I had to stop and reflect. I knew it was only in trusting young people that they could really come through and shine. So often, this had been incredibly successful. But I had to remain so very careful, as we could never have too many fail-safe mechanisms.

His parents were understandably not impressed; nor was the school. It was a setback, but another leadership lesson is that *you can't let setbacks throw you off course*. All procedures were again tightened across the whole of the arts, and we learned not to repeat such a violation.

It was amazing, really, the things we did in the 1990s which would certainly not be allowed today…The very thought of live mercury being used to top up the sign in *Oh What a Lovely War* every evening by the science department makes me shudder even now! The original newsflash sign was fuelled with mercury and flashed headlines across the back of the stage. The sign was a very large oblong box and a powerful aid to the play but it's certainly not something anyone would be allowed to do today! But it created an amazing experience and helped hundreds of young people gain confidence, find their voices, and shine with pride.

Some of my students' learning experiences would get reinforced for me, as I heard about them later.

"Hi. Are you Mr Ullmer?" a voice accosted me in the street many years later. "I was in that amazing show, *Animal Farm*, that you did years ago. It was incredible what you did for the kids, and the time you and the other teachers spent helping us put on the show. It really boosted my confidence, and I'll never forget it."

It was the off-chance comments like this, many years later, that so often reminded me how incredibly worthwhile it all was.

Productions did not, however, always go to plan— showing just how on top of things a leader really must be. I had found an excellent script of Chaucer's *Canterbury Tales*; it stuck very true to the original, with language somewhat shockingly updated. This seemed like another great experience for the students to experience classic literature and show it really could come to life.

If you are familiar with the original *Tales*, you will recall they cover adultery, bare bottoms, coarse language, and a host of other themes with the help of a narrator. I had a range of different groups managing each *Tale*, and I clearly had not fully appreciated the impact of bringing them all together...I remember standing on the balcony, watching the show, and seeing the ribald antics below while wondering, *just what exactly do I have to do to get myself sacked here?*

Fortunately, the head teacher never said anything, and I counted myself very lucky to get away with it! *Good leadership is prepared to take risks*, but I also had to learn that *there are always limits*. I wasn't always able to manage these limits as well as I should have.

Other shows tackled equally strong themes, including working with St Mary's Hospital in Paddington to showcase their play dealing with the consequences of AIDS. It was tackling topics like this, and the honestly which pervaded our drama lessons, that really made young people open up and explore their feelings.

## Pastoral support, therapy and drama productions

Julie was performing a monologue as a task in class about how desperate she felt, and she ended it by speaking about an unnamed person with the quiet words: "Don't you ever

56

f\*\*king well do that to me again." Her delivery was moving and shocking in its intensity. I did what I could to support her in case she wanted to talk more about it, but the situation made me realise how much I really didn't know about the emotions that drama could release. I never discovered what Julie was acting out, but I started to realise how to sensitively refer pupils on to where they could receive expert help when needed.

To build my own understanding and leadership skills in empathy and emotion, I enrolled in a two-year course on the use of the arts in education and therapy. It really helped me come to terms with how every performance or artwork is saying something, and these media can spark discussions of depth and substance. After this course, I felt more ready to deal with the emotions that could surface in class, and I hoped it led me to become a better teacher and listener.

It's an important leadership principle that *you never know it all. There is always more to learn to make you an even better leader and teacher.*

On that note, I made a point of talking to and listening to young people, and drama exercises often helped students unleash hidden demons within. For example, we sometimes performed "waxworks," wherein a student would think of a phrase that someone they didn't like had said to them. It could be something like: "You're useless, and I never want to see you again" or "Why aren't you like your brother? He always gets it right."

The "waxwork" had the job of saying the phrase and standing frozen in the posture of the person who had initially spoken it to the subject. There was an imaginary cord, and when the subject pulled it, the "waxwork" said their line. The subject could make the "waxwork" say the line as often as they wanted, but this time they were in control and got the chance to reply to it whatever they wanted. The responses might include: "Get Lost!" or "You're a calloused, mean person and should be ashamed of yourself."

Some of the replies were even more colourful, but they gave students a chance to find a voice, stand up for themselves in a non-threatening context and reply to things that had stayed on their minds for years. The experience was liberating.

*It's good to get people thinking deeply and appreciating the full depth of the world around them, but it should be balanced with empathy and awareness of the mental needs that students may wish to express.*

I remember the *Canterbury Tales* production for quite another reason too. In my drama exam group, I had one boy called Mike. He usually sat in a corner and was too scared to join in anything. He found it difficult to relate to others, and it was hard work to get him involved.

"Sir, why do I have to do this?" he often asked.

Other times, he was simply silent or cried. He had learning difficulties and struggled with all subjects at the school.

However, I finally managed to persuade him.

"Mike, how about putting a mask on so no one can see you, and try to be part of the horse in *Canterbury Tales*?"

To his credit, he threw himself into it, and his parents were so proud of him.

*We are all part of the same society, and to help others who struggle is one of the most rewarding things we can do, no matter which area or job we are called to work in.* A key focus for me was to find out what a student's particular skills were, and then give them chances to use those skills and flourish.

"Whatever is that dead body doing in the art room?" I asked as I came into the classroom on another occasion. It apparently belonged to a student who was really into latex modelling and visual arts and creating special effects. "You're incredible at doing this," I told him. Then I rewrote the script of the annual production to include a dead body in it.

Similarly, another boy told me about his unicycling skills, and after I told a group how I had learned to fire eat from a local clown, another made a passing comment. He casually mentioned, "I've been practicing my juggling, which I can now do with the juggling sticks on fire…!" Again, I promptly wrote unicycles and fire juggling into the show, and these skills reached a wide and appreciative public audience.

## Outside the box

We took another young person to see a London show with traditional Victorian music hall in it. Before he performed as a music hall compere in an upcoming production, this student was able to see what London shows were really like a hundred years ago.

In the 1990s a lot of staff, particularly in the arts, did a great deal to help young people particularly with extracurricular work. With today's strong focus on academic subjects and exams and the greater distance we now need to keep from students with tighter safeguarding regulations, times have certainly changed. Even then, you had to be careful there will always be one or two people who can misuse the trust that is placed in them.

One young man wanted to set up his own theatre company. He was determined and enthusiastic, and we helped him a lot with both equipment and advice. I once overheard the theatre owner tell him after his latest series of demands, "Do you mind, Terry? This is actually my f\*\*king theatre!" He ended up causing significant trouble in the future, but at the time, it felt great to support him and help him achieve his potential. His team comprised of some students at school along with others who had left or came from other schools. They performed in a variety of places and I even managed to get them a performance at St James' Palace in London. Putting ourselves out for students and helping them achieve great things was not only rewarding for them, but also for the staff around them. They were great times.

On another occasion, Mike, who was Head of Humanities, came to me with a worried expression on his face: "Jonathan, you teach Terry, don't you? He came to me yesterday and demanded the department paid for him to be put on a weekend religious education course with the chief examiner's help to pass his Advanced-level course. He said his teaching had been below par with many absences and he deserved it."

I smiled, knowing how Terry was quite full of himself. "Well, it's up to you," I said, "but if you do it, you need to make sure it's offered to all the students and not just him."

Mike decided to go ahead. A month later, he came back to me to talk about the issue and said, "You'll never guess what he's done now. He's taken a load of books from the course and gone and billed them all to the school!" Terry was not a person who did things by half, and was not interested in taking any prisoners. He was a driven young man, and always had a strong, though not always straightforward, agenda of his own. These were traits I would discover later he clearly took into adult life.

In those days, there were many staff who really went the extra mile to support others. One technology teacher knew of two boys whose father had left home. Since they were not getting fed at lunchtimes, this teacher quietly paid the kitchen to give them free meals. Other staff helped older pupils who had not left school by paying them for babysitting. Another teacher saw an older pupil with a motorbike helmet which looked as if it was about to give up the ghost.

"You're not serious about wearing that, are you?" he said and promptly agreed to give the pupil a new motorbike helmet he still had after giving up biking himself. I often paid for food for students who worked late at night on productions. I recall one student heading for failure in most of his exams and who often truanted. However, he had a real talent for technical sound and lighting work, and often came into school to work late on making it all happen with other students for shows. I remember driving all over the town looking for him when he didn't turn up for his English exams which were really important. However, one thing I did manage to help him achieve: he scored top marks on his lighting and sound capabilities and achieved a grade A in his production work!

These gestures from all the staff sprang from genuine kindness of heart, but as a head teacher later on, I had to strongly advise staff against doing things like this. Sadly, in this day and age, as we will see later, kind gestures can be misinterpreted by others who have sad and unpleasant agendas.

Meanwhile, in the days when we could write and get public exams approved by exam boards, I wrote more than fifteen different exams to test the individual skills of young people. We progressed young people through a wide range of exams that showcased their particular and individual skills— from makeup to design, improvisation to circus skills. The opportunities it gave students were great fun and rewarded them with formal certification for the amazing, hard work they had put in on productions.

Working with a local theatre in the town of Basildon brought great funding opportunities from a government scheme for technical and vocational education. We welcomed three great dancers, artists, and musicians to the school to work with a group of young people taking the new Expressive Arts exams at sixteen years old. I have clear memories of taking a group of fifteen-year-old students out onto the grass by the sports pitches to learn how to do a circular medieval dance, which was somehow part of it all.

It's remarkable what you can get away with when you are enthusiastic and inspire others. The show was called *A Century of Womankind* and told amazing and creative stories covering topics ranging from suffragettes to modern equality issues. For example, we recalled the time when Emily Davison threw herself in front of the king's horse at the famous horse race, the Derby, and killed herself to gain publicity for the cause of "Votes for Women." These women were also notorious for writing "Votes for Women" on the Prime Minister's mirror in his bedroom in Downing Street when they were invited to a reception there with their husbands!

Another time, I recall an artist being very keen on creating structures from what looked like long whippy sticks. The next thing I knew, I heard a scream as I saw one young man grab one and run round, gleefully beating everyone with it. After a few words and great sessions, he become a consummate actor and went on to get high grades in his external examinations. *Sometimes you just need to channel enthusiasm rather than ban it!*

## Not upsetting other staff or your boss!

Events moved from strength to strength, and so did my lessons on leadership. I always tried to keep senior staff fully informed, but clearly, I sometimes overdid things and overloaded them. On one occasion, I was given a long list of swear words which were under no circumstances to be said during the short production of *Bouncers* I was putting on. Some of the words were apparently so disgusting that I hadn't even heard of them. This showed how worried the senior team clearly was about me at times!

I also needed to learn that important lesson that *your boss doesn't want to be given problems; they need solutions.* I was always going to the head to ask for money for various projects and initiatives, and after a while, he got fed up with it. One year when I was doing a large show with nearly three hundred students in at a local priory, as I had done in previous years, I asked for the afternoon off for the final dress rehearsal. This year, the head finally refused. I was really upset, but then I reminded myself that he had the right to do this, and I had to learn to play within his rules. He liked productions, but there was a limit to how much disruption he would allow. I learned my lesson and backed off.

In time, I came to deeply appreciate that I needed to work within the school framework, realising that disruption often wasn't good for the school as a whole. Once I took this on board, relations with senior staff improved. Problems of funding, curriculum, and staff were all desperately important, but many I could solve myself without passing them on. So, I learned to fundraise, obtaining large sums from the National Lottery, Royal Mail, Wimpy, and many others. This paid for key items of equipment we couldn't otherwise afford.

When dealing with problems with staff at Southport Comprehensive School, I always tried to be open and fair, but I clearly made mistakes at times which I regret. However, it did teach me the importance of transparency, openness, and holding fast to my principles. There were times I managed all of this well and times I didn't, but *as you develop your leadership path, it's so important to support others and not say anything behind someone's back you wouldn't say to them directly. Everyone deserves the chance to improve when they get things wron*g. Over the years, I learned to be more gracious and supportive of those around me while still insisting on high standards from students and staff alike.

## The importance of life beyond school

Careers can be all absorbing but there comes a time when priorities have to shift. It was about this time that I led some street theatre at the Edinburgh Fringe Festival and met Jackie, my wife-to-be who was on the drama and dance team. We were both on a team of performers at the famous "fringe," with me helping to lead the drama. We had a great time and a shared love of performing arts, so I asked her to be part of the team that performed in the streets of Salisbury the next year. She even performed as a clown, and I led the improvisation and directed the drama. We hit it off at once.

After we got to know each other better through our time in Salisbury, we returned home in the south of England. I had a request for her: "How about coming to a dinner back at Southend on Sea with me? It will cost you £20, as a group of us are holding the meal to raise money for the church." Jackie only lived an hour away, and it was an easy decision for her to come over.

From such unromantic beginnings, our relationship somehow flourished. Some of my students from the school and the church performed music and drama at the dinner, and there were over twenty different types of cheeses. In fact, the dinner may have cost more to put on than the money we raised, but that didn't seem important. I also had a bet with one of the other organisers that if he got a date from one of the other guests attending, he would donate £100 to the cause. Sadly, he didn't, but I gained many more dates with Jackie, and our love flourished. She shared the zest for life I had seen in my mother and was a practicing midwife and never ceased to get involved in helping others. She was amazing.

At our wedding, former head boy at Southport School, David James, read a lesson, and one of my first Advanced-level drama students was an usher. It mirrored me being one of the ushers at my French teacher's wedding while at school many years before, which had meant a great deal to me and two friends who also took part. We had all studied Advanced-level French together and had great fun while also doing well in our exams.

Our work and home lives blended beautifully. It must have been only weeks after the birth of our daughter, Philippa, that Jackie was on the balcony watching a student-run Shakespeare performance, with our new daughter sleeping soundly in the staff room nearby! We cut the top layer of our wedding cake, which Jackie had hidden in the attic since we married—the fruit cake had matured beautifully—and we ate it with fun and laughter on the balcony of our home in Westcliff. Eighteen months later we were delighted to see the birth of our son, Alex—another great cause for celebration and 'drama' took on a whole new meaning as they both bounced about the house and made the family complete.

*If there's a lesson to be learned here, it's about the importance of developing life and interests outside work and keeping a good work/life balance. People beyond work can bring you the support networks that can prove vital for a happier career and helping you keep going.*

## Breaking new ground

After a while, even the three "witches" in the staff room started to show a human side as I got to know them. I grew to like their raw honesty, which always kept my ego in check!

Later years at Southport School, I found more challenges and opportunities as the arts expanded and grew. It was not long before Advanced-level ("A"-level) Performing Arts was launched for the first time in the UK. We got involved as soon as we could and started the new courses at the school. It took a great deal of determination and drive to set up them up, as numbers of keen students were small, and no school can sustain limitless numbers of uneconomic Advanced-level groups. The arts, however, allowed students to stay at school instead of leaving at sixteen, expanding their range of studies to where they knew they could achieve success.

In early years, we had to deliver the drama and performing arts courses almost entirely outside of school hours, as the school was not prepared to let them run in lesson time, and we had a somewhat unsympathetic head of sixth form. *But if you give up on something you believe in, you will never succeed.* Thus, the pace continued, and young people started signing up for Advanced-level performing arts. One of the most popular areas at this time remained drama, so when a new national A-level drama syllabus was launched, we were quick to seize the opportunity and deliver a course focused on what most of the students at the time were keenest on. As the years went by, it was a delight to see music steadily become more popular, and by the time I left Southport Comprehensive School, it was really flourishing.

At one after-school lesson, two of the older pupils were missing. I had a good idea where they were, so I drove down to the local cricket pitch where I found them playing.

"Haven't you forgotten something?" I called over the pitch at them. Sheepishly, they came off, and I drove them back to their after-school lesson. Honestly, I don't know how we got away with standing firm on lesson attendance, even though it was supposed to be "voluntary." It worked in the end though, as both students went on to get good grades and were very successful.

The leadership lessons and adventures continued, and the results reflected the hard work involved. Sixth-form teaching (sixteen- to eighteen-year-olds) was a whole new ball game, and we had to work hard to put a strong and effective curriculum in place to deliver it. One year, we worked alongside Basildon Theatre again and produced an amazing show about zeitgeist and the 1960s, and we put on a range of workshops involving local primary pupils who loved being in the big shows at the senior school. With new music and art teachers in post with additional drama staff, we were soon running over twenty different kinds of performance events per year—an unheard-of number for any school—and we won a National Drama Award as well as became one of the earliest Artsmark Gold schools in the UK. It was a recognition of excellence in the arts and a great accolade. I became one of the first teachers in the UK to receive performance-related pay in a trial project, and with others, I was filmed teaching and interviewed by the BBC Money Programme. It was an amazing time as exam results for drama and the arts remained high and brought increasing success for many young people.

My leadership skills were growing as I learned to develop my skills, listen to others, encourage ideas to flourish, and go with them.

Having a sixth form required implementing some changes. I felt it was important to treat young people as adults and help them have a real stake in what we were doing. We gave them new access to arts areas and additional responsibilities. We allowed them to work late on productions when there were staff in the building, and we offered as much support as possible. But there were challenges along the way.

Homophobia was rife in the school, and boys taking drama were particularly at risk; I also had always been targeted because of my "posh" accent. I remember in early days; I overheard two students talking.

"Who's that, then?"

"That's Ullmer, the new drama teacher."

"Well, he must be gay then. All drama teachers are gay!"

This was the only time, as a straight man, that I had heard this kind of thing, and it made me sensitive to older students who also faced it and other such discrimination. One person openly, if only jokingly, referred to the older drama students as "poncers and mincers." We had to be very supportive of these students to keep them confident and on task. I often let them use my office and drama areas at break and lunchtime to provide a safe haven, which seemed to help.

## Treating others with respect

For particularly talented students, I organised work experience with a theatre group at Ringwood in Hampshire to stay with a theatre in education company. As my aunt worked at the Old Vic, a top London theatre, I tried hard to get them work experience there, but sadly to no avail. I just had to keep going.

I also ran a drama group at the local Baptist church, where we were able to do some quite innovative work involving young students as well as those who had left school or were at university. I published a book of their sketches, which came out of a lot of improvised fun! David, the former head boy, now at university, was particularly fun to work with doing this; while playing the part of an irritating child, I remember him uttering the immortal lines, "What happens if I lick my fingers and stick them in this electric light socket?"

Lines were often blurred, as we worked not just in school but also across the local community with wide ranges of people from primary school staff to local pubs and theatres. Past students who had been involved in TV or the arts since schooldays came back for a photo shoot to support us with the local press. Beyond school, I was known often as "Jonathan" or "the guv'nor," but back at Southport School during the day, I made sure to conform to policy and was officially "Mr Ullmer." *Fitting in with the school and institutions is important, as you must respect the rules and particular expectations of the school that employs you. And when you try to bring about change, it's important to do so in a respectful manner. Remember, the school was there before you were…*

The changes I did bring about mostly involved raising expectations and demanding that we challenge students to do their very best.

"Sir, why do we have to take our mock drama exams in Southport High Street?" an agonised student pleaded.

"Well, if you can perform there in front of strangers in the street, any other speaking you must do to others will be easy!" I replied. So, I got a council licence, and from teaching Commedia dell 'Arte, the masked students entertained shoppers with a wide range of mime, acting, and song. The result really was quite amazing! It just goes to show that if you set expectations really high, people will grab at them. I would calmly tell them each year where the exams would be held, so the varied location ended up as a kind of "given." I recall occasions of putting far too much in my mini metro car, complete with students, to get to a High Street performance.

To my enduring incomprehension, none of the students told me *where to get off*. Yet these young people felt extremely free to share their opinions…!

On one hand, this was about giving students autonomy and treating them as adults, but it leads to a key leadership principle: *You must treat all those around you, almost at all ages, with respect. Do not patronise them. When you trust and encourage people, letting them go with their ideas and supporting them to do their best, it's amazing what they can do.*

The other teaching aspect I learned to feel strongly about, with clear links to leadership, was the flourishing of creativity and critical thinking. I enjoyed taking young people to see the National Theatre Production of *Wind in the Willows*. It was an extravaganza of light and colour with rotating stages rising up and down—creating rivers, woods, and homes—along with Toad's car driving merrily along while tooting its horn. The show appealed to the sense of spectacular and the imagination, and was a festival of creativity.

The students couldn't understand why they had to sit in set places in the theatre, as many of them were then used to sitting wherever they liked in the local cinema. However, trying to make people think in new and different ways, and showing them things beyond the imagination, helped foster creativity—without which very few of our great inventors would have succeeded. It also made me remember the words of my long-serving head of art on his retirement: "The flourishing of the arts is the mark of a civilised society." He was certainly right, and with students voluntarily working well into the evenings on productions, a real sense of teamwork was created. With new friends made, people found they could do more than they ever thought possible.

To emphasise the impact that these principles can have, a student from my years at Southport School sent me an email completely out of the blue, much later in 2015. It read:

Good morning, Jonathan. I believe I haven't seen you since you left Southport School. I don't know if you remember me as a pupil, but throughout my secondary schooling, I was involved in the technical team which you created to run the lighting and sound for productions at the school. I fully understand if you don't accept the friend request I have sent. After all, I am a former pupil and haven't seen you in fourteen years. I just wanted to take this opportunity to thank you for running that after-school club. Your direct involvement has led me to have an amazing career in theatre, which I am very thankful of. If you are ever passing theatres in London, it would be great to thank you in person. I hope you are well and life has been treating you good.
Many thanks,
Rob

I remembered him, along with so many others, well. He gave a great deal to support the students who took "up front" roles, and behind the scenes helped make so much possible. I was delighted to accept his friend request, and many other students from the period have also kept in touch over the years.

I only had strong negative feedback from one of these many thousands of students—one who hadn't really fulfilled his potential and looked for a number of other people to scapegoat in rather unpleasant ways. Unfortunately, he was also a journalist and took every opportunity to exploit this.

*Don't get so caught up in the world of ambition, publicity and greed that you fail to see where the real value often is. When you trust young people, enthusing and giving them responsibility and encouragement regardless of personal cost, you get so much more back in return. You don't do some of the best things in life for pay or money; when you give your time freely, in years to come, you can often see how it was worth every minute.*

The technical club operated every Tuesday night from 5:00 to 8:00 p.m. and often later, as young people supported and helped train each other in computer lighting and sound systems while creating amazing effects. I wouldn't swap these years for anything. They were incredible. I realised towards the end of my time at the school that over 75% of students there had taken part in some kind of public performance. It was many years later that I would come to realise that many of these young people, as adults, had written to Buckingham Palace, about me to praise the work I had done for them, and more was yet to come in the future…

*It is a key function of leadership to support others. The arts are not for a talented minority—they are for all, and every student should have the chance to take part. We don't live in an isolated bubble, and great leaders are known for their supportive work with others beyond the immediate workplace. Doing this involves valuing all aspects of life— and sharing the message that you value others. This shows you aren't solely driven by the close and immediate, but you care beyond this as well.*

## Developing your leadership skills

- **Never give in**. When one door shuts, another will open. You must watch for it.
  There are always ways to solve problems you face, and when you can't see what they are, seek good people to discuss and brainstorm them with you.
- **Always show respect**. Treat young people as adults, and you will in most cases find the youth will act like them. Respect people who you don't like or disagree with; this will help your relationships to no end. Find things to praise and say good things about people. You will be surprised how much doing so transforms relationships.
- **Support others**. See the agendas other people have and help them achieve their goals. By giving strong support, you will often find that when you need that support returned, it will come from the most unexpected quarters. If you are known to help and support others, people will talk, and it will be known. Make a point of helping difficult colleagues or students.
- **Break down barriers between the school and community**. There can be great lessons in getting older students to help younger ones at other schools, as well as to help the elderly or others in the community. Working with others in this way

encourages an idea of service and makes young people, and the adults around them, better people while encouraging mutual support. Some of my best friends came from local schools where I got my students to work with the younger pupils.

- **Never think you know it all.** All of us, no matter what stage of our career, must keep learning. It really is a lifelong process. Look for ways to extend your knowledge, teaching skills, and expertise—there are always many opportunities out there.

# Chapter 4
# Dealing with Poor Leadership

*On board a sinking ship...*

The head teacher at Southport School was excellent; he spoke the language of the pupils, inspired the staff, and resolutely moved the school forward. He also had the foresight to appoint key senior leaders who were able to deliver what he couldn't. A highly competent deputy ensured the school won awards and had the flair to put together successful bids, and his appointments at the middle leadership level, and the responsibility he gave them, ensured the school moved forward in a wide range of areas. But under the surface, the possibility of change was brewing.

Another deputy, who was an excellent mentor, had a long chat with me in his office one day.

"You're working really hard, Jonathan. But just stop and think and ask yourself if you can be working at this pace for the next ten years. What you're doing is a young man's job. Running twenty shows a year and using the amount of energy and determination which you do really isn't sustainable. You need to think hard about your next career steps."

This was incredibly wise advice, and he was completely right.

This kind of mentoring and friendly advice is vital in leadership in helping staff move forward and be fulfilled in their posts. *A job that neglects formal mentoring arrangements is a dead end and does not encourage strong and powerful leadership.* I was never one to rest on my laurels, and now that I had a theatre and a thriving arts area, it did seem like the right time to move to new challenges. I had spent over twelve years at the school, and I realised I really couldn't keep going at the same pace. It seemed a good time to start looking for the next step in my career. *It's time to go*, I told myself.

Is it crucial to have a good head teacher or CEO to learn from? My next appointment gave alarming insights into what happens when you don't have a strong leader to set the tone and ensure that targets are both achievable and delivered.

The new principal at the next college, where I became assistant principal, was a person of determination and action. Working in an area of Suffolk where people seemed to know the cost of everything and the value of nothing, the school needed to be clear and determined, with strong vision. It had a great track record of doing so, so it didn't seem like a difficult task for them to continue.

As they quoted from Disney and a wide range of educational thinkers, the new principal had the strategy all mapped out, inspiring all those they came into contact with. They talked much about "twenty-first century education," and the "untold possibilities" that existed out there. It was certainly true that leadership roles were growing all over the Western World and that the days of low-skilled work were quickly coming to an end. This principal believed in the future.

When I was interviewed for a new post as assistant headteacher in charge of marketing and publicity, alongside teaching English and drama at their school, the principal seemed to be the real deal. They promptly set up new structures, changed "heads of year" to "learning directors," grouped subjects together, and had a vision for becoming a college of science and technology. Their contact list was impressive, and as a powerful networker, the principal called in people from the highest positions in their field to help make an impact. People at the school started noticeably using their phraseology. This was the strength of the vision: everyone felt part of something rather big.

*The ability to inspire and enthuse others is a key leadership trait.* You don't need to be as charismatic as this principal was, but you do need a clear vision which you can communicate. It goes back to Ezekiel in the Bible: "Where there is no vision, the people perish" (Proverbs 29:18). A clear plan of action and way ahead helps inspire others, and you must be well organised and articulate with this vision.

Soon I was at work—monitoring press coverage, overseeing publications, taking charge of education strategy for eleven- to fourteen-year-olds, and organising effective displays in school and the community. I was in my element. I enjoyed being called into key meetings and discussing ideas, and we felt like a strong team.

Those who refused to come on board, on the other hand, were looked down on as limited and uninspired. And it was surmised that those with similar ideas must be clearly be copying us.

I listened hard to one of their inspiring talks to parents about how the school was moving forward and how the future was "ours to grasp." I also listened to the principal speaking to staff as they outlined their vision of what had been achieved in the first hundred days.

But something worried me. Decisions seemed to be made in small groups or cliques, and the school didn't have the feel of inclusiveness. The seductive vision didn't seem to be matching up to reality. Soon I had those very learning directors that had been appointed asking me exactly what their new roles were and how they differed from their old ones? The theory that they would add overseeing data and educational attainment to their former pastoral role was great, and it mirrored what the best schools were doing. But on the ground, people hadn't been trained and didn't know what their jobs were. And the structures to underpin these big changes simply weren't in place.

This was vision without substance. There was a failure of leadership and the work that had to go on behind the scenes to make change possible. Such transformation simply had not been done. For example, there was clearly talent in the school, but it had not been harnessed in the right direction, roles were confused, and the nitty gritty of hard work to make visions become reality was absent.

To reinforce my thoughts that things weren't running smoothly, one inspector who had been in school to check up on progress, and who was employed by the principal to report back to them, took me to one side. He conspiratorially and rather misogynistically muttered, "Great person, your principal. Very impressive vision. Sadly, fur coat, no knickers…" This statement was meant to reinforce that for all the charisma, they lacked the underpinning of ability and hard work.

A grand plan was hatched for quality assurance, overseen by a new consultant. Rather than simply control quality with checkpoints, there would be an ongoing process of improvement. This was meant to ensure that the school moved forward constantly, and that we were all inspired to reach excellence in practice. Teams of paid consultants were assigned to come in to review a particular area of the school and make recommendations. Lessons were to be observed, and departmental records and structures were to be investigated and reviewed as part of this process of continuous improvement.

At a dinner with the consultants the night before they began their work—it was clear wining and dining were an important part of this process—they spoke informally to key leaders involved in the area. The next day, they set to work.

Unfortunately, although the agenda behind their assignment was to advise on continuous improvement, I felt the effect was often to encourage staff to move on and show up deficiencies in the school. The consultants did not pull their punches. They graded teachers in the same way one might grade turkeys, destroying confidence and vision in the process. A number of staff and departments were told they were failing, and the continuous improvement soon felt as if it had degraded into a hatchet job—affecting me as well. I had been told to teach a subject outside my area of expertise and duly followed the lesson plans I was given to make it happen, only to have the lesson rated as unsatisfactory, with me written off as a weak teacher.

*Quality assurance is a key way to move institutions forward, but you do not inspire and enthuse staff to do better by telling them how bad they are.* Even the UK government has now moved away from grading teachers, realising it simply does not have the desired aim.

As a result of this experience, some staff who had been unsupported felt the ground pulled from under them. They had been lulled into a false sense of security with cosy dinners, and then as their reward were to be pulled to pieces by the critique which followed.

An unfortunate consequence when these kinds of things happen is that a rather toxic atmosphere can develop leading to a 'dog eat dog' situation as staff seek either to bolster their own position or remain true carriers of the "vision."

What people were crying out for was a supportive mentoring process—a process whereby they could discuss their work and reflect on it while coming up with changes in a non-threatening and non-confrontational manner. What they got were formal written reports saying how bad they were, and a one-off grade which may or may not have reflected their years of effort in the classroom.

Meanwhile the school pressed on with its bid for science and technology status. I was put in charge of writing this as a drama teacher, yet there was no extra professional help offered to me at all. I consulted with all the stakeholders, but they also had not been briefed or trained. Their ideas lacked originality or flair, as they had never been shown the possibilities available to them. In the circumstances, we did as well as we could; but it was never going to cut the mustard, as our leader had neither trained nor prepared us for this work.

The blame game then started. Although I was protected by my line manager who gamely took the fall for me, it was hardly his fault.

The principal then took over managing the bid themselves and finally engaged with it all to try to make it happen. They, however, called in a range of experts from all over the country to help write the bid and ensure it had the pazazz and flair it needed to be successful. Some staff felt the targets appeared to be somewhat optimistic, but with the expertise and training provided, no doubt along with much ghost-writing, the new bid was finally completed. Finally, it was submitted and received a far more favourable response, and the school was approved by the government to become a college of science and technology.

I was put in charge of rebranding the school with a new name, and I spent much time checking that the name suggested wasn't linked to a medieval brothel or carrying any negative connotations which had been missed. Managing the project properly, I called in a designer I knew with expertise, and we worked together to involve staff and listen to all stakeholders carefully. After proper training, preparation, and engagement of experts to support us, I headed the project with considerable success. When the new logo was unveiled, it met with universal approval from staff, the school board, and students. It clearly paid homage to the past while looking to the future—with careful design so it could be reproduced at any size and still look sharp and convincing. Many logos simply fail because they can't be sized up or down, or look good on clothing; I wanted to ensure all bases were covered, and the new designs were well and truly fit for purpose.

Despite the success of our logo redesign, the school, was increasingly failing both staff and students. Things steadily went downhill.

"Are you happy with the way things are going?" I was asked by a friendly governor after an evening meeting.

I was silent.

Then suddenly the retiring deputy head who was with me piped up. "The school is heading for failure at inspection. It's getting really bad, and I can't tolerate it any longer."

The genie was out of the bottle, and I finally opened up. "It's getting harder and harder to see the school going downhill. Something must be done to stop it," I confessed.

We were aware that the chair of the governing body seemed to be living in a state of complete denial. He was photographed for an article in the local paper which stated the school was "sailing on a sea of excellence." It was getting increasingly difficult to square this with what was actually happening in the school, as standards continued to fall.

In public and with the governors, the principal was completely in charge of their brief and remained convincing and inspiring. However, it became increasingly difficult to cover up the lack of planning, preparation, and support that was clearly needed in the background. I worked hard on the strategy for eleven- to fourteen-year-olds (the Key Stage 3 strategy), but a consultant was called in to rubbish what we were doing. It was part of the way the "quality assurance" process seemed to work.

"No one has heard of this KS3 strategy," the consultant told me. "It's non-existent and having no impact." He had made a point of listening to gossip in the negative atmosphere that prevailed at the school.

"Well, did you ask people about the changes to lessons plans we made or the launch of detailed schemes of work and department audits?" I asked. They were all part of the strategy but didn't have the KS3 strategy name on them on them, as the whole approach was to support teachers and departments through the whole school while helping them move forward. "Have you seen the posters in English classrooms about how to do non-fiction writing? Or the posters up about questioning skills?" These components had all formed part of this initiative. But the consultant wasn't interested.

As had become usual, facts were immaterial. I was not on an ego trip about what I was in charge of; it was about helping others. The KS3 strategy was so well embedded that we hadn't really referred to it by this name, as if this was something different. The strategy was about departments improving systems and was becoming part of our practice. I designed new register lists with clear and ready access to the latest data on every student to inform lesson planning, a new lesson plan proforma was rolled out, and department audits took place to encourage heads of department to review and analyse results and what they had done to set meaningful and relevant targets. However, the consultant seemed to be interested in finding fault, and the principal had little concept of what the strategy was about. It felt as if they hadn't attended the relevant meetings or training, and told senior staff they didn't understand much about it. Hence, it appeared to have little value.

What was happening seemed so sad. At times I didn't know where to turn. I was incredibly lucky to work closely with a deputy principal, who was the most competent and experienced person I had ever had the opportunity to learn from. I picked up a great deal from our conversations; he showed me not only by example, but also through effective mentoring how things can be done well. *Strong and supportive mentoring is essential in leadership to help people move forward and achieve their potential.*

As the senior team learned to cope with being on board a sinking ship, we did our best to keep it afloat as long as possible. I on many evenings met over a pint with the deputy principal as we talked about what to do and how to mitigate the effects of what was happening to the staff and students.

"I can't believe those targets set for the school," I sighed in exasperation at the local pub. "And today I discovered the Key Stage 3 funding appears to have been spent along with the money earmarked for our work with the middle school." The principal was well within their rights to do this, but I just hadn't been told about this at all. The school continued to run a large deficit.

The deputy headteacher sympathised as he lit yet another cigarette.

"The action plan by the IT consultant has been ditched and targets have been changed, so we really don't know where we stand. Trouble is, the targets aren't based on anything…" he replied. We had to just try and make things work, but some at the very top seemed to be living in a world of their own with little relation to what was happening on the ground. *The leaders at the top hold all the trump cards, and it can be incredibly hard to change things without their support.*

To cement our friendships, one of the friendly consultants—who had really hit it off with us all and understood the good work we were doing—got hold of a pair of golden balls from somewhere, held together with ribbon. I have no idea where they came from. Each week, senior staff would nominate someone to receive the "Golden Balls" for something they had done to make things better for the school in spite of the situation we were in with the top leaders. This exercise provided a moment of fun and distraction in a tense and serious situation. If we made a formal complaint about things, it could be seen at best as disloyal, and at worst, as insubordinate—clearly putting our jobs at risk.

The bursar did stand up to the principal very firmly and told the governors what they saw happening. This then moved into a "me or them" position with the principal and governors. In these situations, the principal almost always wins, so the bursar lost their job for their forthrightness. We knew we had to play it all carefully, or we would go the same way.

The Golden Balls were a great distraction, but one day, the principal found out about them. The cat was out of the bag about our Golden Balls game, so they were banned… Meanwhile the world at school moved on with no end in sight to this tension.

However, slowly, governors started to realise that things were awry. At the end of one of the sub-committee meetings, at which the principal was not present, I and another senior member of staff could no longer remain silent. We spoke out in confidence to the governors present, trusting they would not let it go further. This may have been one of the events which caused a number of governors to start questioning and wondering about what was happening.

After that meeting, I was interviewed individually by a governor I worked with and trusted. It was dangerous territory for the senior staff, but an area we had to walk into. No one could deny that the school was in serious difficulty and heading quickly to being put into special measures if we had an inspection. The time for action had arrived. Results were falling, targets were not being met, and even the teaching staff had started to question the vision and what was going on.

Finally, the school board outvoted their chair—the one who had talked about us "sailing on a sea of excellence"—and the principal lost their job after a vote of no confidence. It was a relief to see it all happen, and the school was able to move on. However, with the same school board in place, another mistake in appointments would soon happen...

After an interim period, the new principal arrived. He introduced a system of giving staff a lapel pin to wear when they had been graded as "good" In a lesson observation. I can't think of a worse way to demotivate staff than to make it publicly clear who were thought of as "good" teachers and who were clearly not.

When he came to my lesson, I felt so intimidated. I didn't get the gold star, which seemed to confirm his opinion of me. Fortunately, when we later had a mock inspection, a member of Her Majesty's inspectorate with over ten years of experience, rated my teaching as "outstanding." I got my gold star, but still felt it was an unfair and humiliating system.

I was soon asked to be part of a team that was responsible for something called the "Four Counties Project." I led much of the work for what was a government initiative to boost external exam results. I worked hard behind the scenes to analyse student grades and see what we could learn from them.

Initially the school had encouraged better results by getting each department to lay out its plans to support young people—including after-school sessions, new resources, better lesson planning. That didn't work. It had little impact on students, and it was clear that a far more focused approach was needed.

From this unsuccessful approach, we worked on a very clear targeting of data which identified exactly who the students were who were at risk of not passing certain subjects. Specific staff were engaged in the issues with particular students, and strategies were agreed to moving forward. This approach was highly individual and sometimes involved students dropping subjects to focus time where it was needed.

Helping each at-risk student develop their own individual action plan seemed to make a difference. We were the only national project that raised attainment, and results went up by 12 percent. Tighter control of exam entry procedures similarly raised results by 10 percent, while saving £40,000 through efficiencies.

*The key leadership lesson here is that hard work behind the scenes and working alongside others can really bring results.*

Meanwhile, in spite of all this, the school hurtled towards a failing grade by the government, and the inevitable inspection confirmed this. The staff were demotivated, and parents who had sent their children from out of area to the school suddenly realised they had far better schools near them. School numbers started to fall in an area which already had too many secondary schools, and the situation looked serious. One of the key leadership mistakes had been made of failing to inspire and engage staff.

*Without proper mentoring and training in place and an atmosphere that lacked vision, direction, and empathy, the school's days were numbered. If only leadership had engaged staff, listened to teachers and students, and supported them while also challenging and inspiring them, all of this could have been so easily avoided.*

However, just as things couldn't get worse, the principal moved on following the inadequate rating for the school. He was replaced by an outstanding deputy principal.

"We're going to work together to move the school forward," he told us at his first staff meeting. In that session, he set out a clear vision, and everyone was able to discuss what we thought a great school looked like. The tone had completely changed. Suddenly, staff were appreciated and encouraged, genuine support was provided, and we started to feel like a team again. We were inspired and felt included.

At his first assemblies, students were also encouraged and supported from the top down. As a result of these changes, the school started to improve.

*It is amazing just how much the tone of an institution is set from the top.* Slowly, a new positivity enveloped the whole school. People—even senior staff—who had been affected by the demoralising effect of being in a failing school, started to reflect a new positive ethos. The change in staff took root. There were of course the few teachers who would retain their cynicism and unpleasantness, but they were far outmatched by those reflecting a new tone and vision. It became a pleasure to go to school, as we knew we were going to be supported and encouraged, and were clearly part of a team to move things forward.

The sense of teamwork included everyone, including students. The new head teacher planned to set up student councils with proper leadership training. One of their conferences in the future was to be set in a national football ground!

While I enjoyed teaching English, media studies, and drama, I even had former students who had gone on to university come back and run workshops for the students. We had the former editor of *the Sunday Sport* come to talk about journalism, and a drama student ran workshops on alternative theatre. We created great films and helped students analyse and find their voices. The English department was incredibly supportive, and working there was a pleasure.

*Leadership does not, however, only involve the people at your school. Great leadership moves beyond to embrace the local community and beyond and helps young people see their place in a broader community.*

I was delighted to take on the new responsibility for creating "Citizenship and Enterprise Days" across the school. It was incredibly hard work to design a timetable for nearly one thousand students for a whole day, but we had the army running teamworking sessions, banks teaching financial literacy, along with British Gas, the Rifle Range, local employers, and more. Lessons were provided on CVs and applications, while Young Enterprise and a wide range of other organisations worked with young people to help them become independent decision-makers. We had an external group work on presentations for job interviews, with mock interviews by local employers offered for a whole year group. In-house projects were undertaken, with students working in new ways with new teams.

A sense of purpose flowed through the days. as we focused on different ways of doing things and creative thinking. This proved to offer excellent leadership training. For example, students planning buildings and airports allowed for real flair to develop, and budgeting introduced ideas of enterprise and reality into the concepts.

*Collapsing the timetable for a whole day like this allows for new and different things to be done outside the curriculum, and a focus on citizenship and enterprise is an excellent way to do it. Schools often offer wonderful ideas for the few, but by collapsing the timetable you can create memorable activities for everyone and foster a real sense of inclusion.*

*It's vital in a successful school or organisation to encourage new ways of thinking and break up the usual continuity of things now and again. This can bring fresh thinking and variety, and companies can often use this to motivate and enthuse staff.*

It is of course the cruellest irony that just as things were on a firm upward trajectory, pupil numbers continued to fall. The label of "inadequate" cast its pall and was not readily forgotten by the community. In spite of excellent work with local schools, great teaching, and an encompassing vision to involve everyone, redundancies were inevitable. It is perhaps tribute to the skill and inclusivity of the newly named head teacher, that the school still held together as people were losing their jobs. The senior team that I was a key member of under the new head teacher soon pulled the school out of special measures, and it became a thriving and increasingly successful school with a dynamic and happy staff.

However, in spite of ongoing success, numbers continued to fall, and the size of the senior team had to shrink again. For the second time, I had to apply for my own job in a re-structure. This time I would be competing against an outstanding woman who had led the attendance strategy. It felt so sad that one of us would have to lose our jobs when we had both worked so hard and seen such great results.

The time had come to move on, so I applied for other jobs in earnest. Meanwhile the school went on to achieve outstanding inspection results and submitted a bold and ambitious bid to become a vocational centre, which was desperately needed in the area.

However, the political flavour was moving firmly in favour of "free schools," which were set up by local groups with a lot of independence from regulations. The bid for the vocational centre was turned down and political drive overcame common sense. The old school had to close, and a proud history of community support and attempts at genuine innovation and excellence came to a sad end.

## Lessons for overcoming bad leadership

- **Inspire others with clear vision and planning**. It's vital for head teachers and senior staff to share a vision when work begins. The best senior staff I know took time to discuss ideas with teachers and help shape hearts and minds. A great way of doing this is to have a session with teaching staff on what makes an ideal school. The senior team can then work with these ideas from the teachers to craft a vision. Then, most important of all, you must work hard to ensure that words become concrete actions, and people are supported to follow through. Strategy must not be just empty words.

- **Make sure everyone knows their role**. Clear job descriptions must underpin jobs which are relevant, up-to-date, and helpful. Each role should have the school vision clearly articulated within it. You can then use these descriptions to help set relevant targets with staff in an effective system of performance management, which helps fulfil the vision of the school. There are great online systems available to help ensure the voices of teachers as well as senior staff are heard, and that targets are genuinely agreed. Then it's vital to ensure that everyone knows their role and is fully involved in the way forward.

- **Moving forward does not involve denigrating others**. This is an obvious point, but one that is sadly often missed. One head teacher I worked with constantly denigrated his predecessor, and it really didn't feel good. You don't make yourself look better by rubbishing others. Good leaders look for ways to help and support others to ensure they succeed. They don't put their staff down. On this note, think hard before you say anything negative about others; it will almost certainly rebound.

- **Be aware of who holds the cards**. It's very difficult to do things without the support of those above you. You may win a skirmish and then lose the war. Tread carefully.

# Chapter 5
# Turning Around a Failing School

*For the first time in my life, I oversaw the*
*confiscation of a Porsche…*

Sometimes in your career, the time comes to look differently at what you have been doing. I began to wonder if a mid-life career change was in order after everything I had experienced, so I went to consult with a career advisor in London.

"What exactly do you want to do, Jonathan?" she asked me. "Have you ever thought of working in the independent school sector?"

"But why on earth would any kind of prestigious school want to appoint me? I've just been part of a team that has led a failing school out of special measures!"

It really hadn't entered my head that, actually, a lot of independent schools are failing. They just don't advertise the fact; it's hidden behind glossy brochures and misleading statistics.

I took her advice and applied for the headship of a top international college in London. To my even greater surprise, I was one of the final two candidates. It appeared that my experiences in helping to turn around failing schools was a positive factor in my favour. I didn't get the job, but to have been taken so seriously certainly gave me food for thought. So, when I saw a similar style advertisement for a vice principal at an independent Oxford sixth-form college, I called my career advisor—who I realised had handled appointments for this school in the past—to ask if they were handling this one. They weren't, but the latest advertisement simply followed the template she had previously used. It was rather cheeky, but I applied knowing I now had a referee who knew the principal of the college.

I was a rank outsider, but with a known referee, I became less of a risk. The other candidates were typical of those from the independent sector and probably had little idea about how to turn round schools or what the latest in education theory and change management was.

"So how would you go about raising results in the college?" I was asked.

I spoke to the interview panel about the difference between quality control and quality assurance, which underpinned strong schools, and how I could bring real difference to young people. It had slowly dawned on me that the independent sector, contrary to government pronouncements, is actually far behind good state schools in policy and practice. They are highly successful because they generally have hard-working, motivated young people, and they simply throw out anyone who doesn't follow the rules or achieve results. I also had gained a great deal of experience in change management, having been part of a team that had turned round a failing school. I knew clearly by this stage what things needed to be done.

I nervously awaited the outcome. Unlike in the state sector, you don't get a reply on the same day as the interview if you are to be appointed, and it was some considerable time before I heard back again. This is probably not a bad thing, as it gives people time to discuss candidates fully. And without the pressure of a single day to appoint, they are probably less likely to make expensive mistakes.

I finally got the call and was offered the job. I was in shock! This really was a major change, as I left the security of the Teacher's Pension Scheme and the highly regulated world of state education and launched into something relatively unknown.

The key leadership lesson from it all is that *success has far more to do with you as a person, and less to do with your previous experience*. It wasn't hard to read up on regulations for boarding school standards and the independent school inspection system, and I quickly became an expert on what was expected. What I brought to the post was a determination to meet each of these standards and help create a unified college with clear purpose. Little did I know what exactly I had let myself in for…

I looked with amazement as the college prepared to welcome students of over fifty nationalities arriving from all areas of the globe. They were coming to take Advanced-level courses to prepare them for entry into top UK universities. It was fast-paced and fun, as I saw boarding houses made ready and staff busy preparing for the New Year. A new house system was just being introduced, in line with many UK private schools.

I soon met a bewildered group of four heads of houses, in charge of pupil welfare, who asked me, "Jonathan, what exactly is our role, and just what are we expected to do?"

I met with the bemused group and listened to what they had to say about the college, and swiftly forged their role with them. I had to think fast and on my feet.

We met regularly to talk about what was happening, and they were a mine of information about what was going on. It was soon apparent that rules on curfews and age-appropriate restrictions simply weren't in place, a significant number of staff were unqualified and often doing their own thing, and levels of supervision were extremely weak. I then discovered more about past goings-on, with stories of inappropriate relations between staff and students, the possible extent of drug use in the college, and the problems with installing a systematic disciplinary framework. Systems that were in place were often inconsistent or not understood and ranged from the draconian to the laissez faire. Random drugs-testing had been introduced to attempt to cut down on the drugs issue at the college, but there was no personal development or training support for young people to show them there was an alternative to substance misuse when under pressure.

*It's important to tackle issues, but even more important to look at and deal with the underlying issues which make things happen.*

To be fair, the headteacher had only been in post a year and was fighting to catch up.

Further discussions with the new heads of house took place as we slowly unpicked what must be done and the issues the college was facing. We were not compliant with attendance reporting, welfare, safeguarding, and a range of issues. HR files did not meet regulations concerning a single central register of appointments and many policies simply weren't in place. The college appeared to have been operating outside many of the norms of educational practice. What really put the icing on the cake was that in the first half of my first term there, I discovered a student had gone missing for almost three weeks, and no one appeared to have known about it.

The college had founded its reputation on being informal—a place that would accept UK students who didn't fit in with a formal private school education—and what I was finding proved that, up to now, it had a very much "laissez-faire" approach indeed.

I took a deep breath in my office and realised if the Department for Education walked in right then, there was little doubt in my mind we could have been closed. However, *there is no place for panic in situations like this*. There were issues, and we were going to create effective teams to deal with them.

Each time I met with the heads of houses, new issues were arising, and we simply couldn't do everything at once. However, I discovered a core group of people who really cared and had been extremely worried by what had been going on.

There is no such thing as a "super head" or "super deputy head." Instead, it's all about getting groups of people to pull together and work as a team to bring about institutional change. This is an impossible job for one person, but when groups of people join together, all playing their own part, then progress really starts to happen. The journey we needed to take was really amazing, and you would never believe the details if I made them up…

"Why are our students driving Porsches and other fast cars?" I was asked one day. "Students at the college aren't supposed to have cars—have you any idea what's going on?"

One group of students had been working with gangs in London to get hold of nice cars by using fake IDs, insurance cards, and driving licences. So, we had students driving illegally, and no doubt erratically, all over Oxford.

For the first time in my life, I oversaw the confiscation of a Porsche! A great deal of work went on in the background to break up the criminal rings, and the principal was in his element working on it. I was also later to discover there was an extortion racket going on with older students taking protection money from younger ones.

"We'll get these gangs sorted and clear this all up," he promised. I stood back in amazement and focused on sorting out what needed to be put in place for what could be a formal inspection at any moment…There really was never a dull moment!

On another occasion, it was reported to me that a photography teacher had inadvertently let students take unclothed pictures of each other. And another time, I discovered that the university entrance officer, to his credit, had refused a bribe of £11,000 to falsify references.

Then I had a knock on my office door.

"Jonathan, the king is waiting to see you downstairs…"

It was indeed a Nigerian king; the clientele we dealt with were as remarkable as their offspring.

For each industrious student, there were others who treated the school as a holiday camp and turned up to lessons as and when they pleased. Of course, there were no strong attendance records, so no one had really noticed before.

We had to move fast and effectively to deal appropriately with the issues thrown at us. But we also had to keep our eyes firmly fixed on the strategic issues of building systems, approaches, and staff buy-in, which would prevent any of these things from happening again.

The next thing I quickly had to turn my attention to was the quality of teaching. We clearly had some excellent staff, but many others were part-timers from other local colleges who had not been trained. Their teaching practice resembled that which I'd experienced at school nearly forty years ago.

The difficulty was not only that young people had changed so much over the years, as had their method of learning, but also that our knowledge of the brain had grown so much. We knew much more about how people learn effectively.

We had to couple this with the fact that vast numbers of our students did not have English as their first language. For many of them, their parents had heard of UK education and how it encouraged critical thinking and creativity, and they wanted it for their children. The old ways of "chalk and talk," though replaced with "whiteboard and marker pen," simply didn't cut it. It wasn't the fault of the teachers; I soon discovered that many of them had not had the opportunity or support to do things differently. In fact, many teachers worked in their own little worlds, with little in terms of schemes of work or teamwork, and they were taking on massive burdens which often really weren't necessary.

The first task was to start providing clear and effective staff training while increasing the numbers of full-time staff, so we could guarantee they were around to receive the support they needed. There had been seven full-time staff when I started, and this soon increased to over thirty. We held training days on basic techniques, and I introduced them to the three-part lesson—starter, main body, and plenary. It wasn't essential or necessary to teach in this format, but for staff who needed help in seeing different ways of doing things, it was a lifeline.

The shift in teaching during this period had been away from "teaching," and it being graded like a performance, and towards "learning," focused on how much students in the lesson actually learned. It was a pretty major shift and involved the teacher checking on learning regularly to ensure everyone was on board.

Many sessions were therefore held on teaching and learning techniques, and crucially, some of the staff were involved in delivering them. We had to aim at ownership of ideas and staff talking together to share what worked for them.

*It's no good just to have outsiders or new people telling others what to do; people must see it from the people they work alongside as well.*

We launched training in a wide range of areas, along with tours of the boarding houses, so staff could see and understand more about where they were working. Relationships started to form between house supervisors and other staff as they realised, they were on the same team and wanted to work together.

New staff training was launched, so teachers new to the profession who came to work with us could see the aims and ethos of the college while being supported and helped through their initial terms at the school. An exemplary member of staff led the training and initiated an excellent programme.

The school was expanding, and we needed staff from all directions, including those fresh from training college. The key was starting to get people to feel that they were part of something, and not just a group of individuals who came and went without seeing others. We introduced staff briefings and newsletters, along with booklets to help staff in their day-to-day work.

However, *top-down initiatives will only go so far. There must be wider and greater involvement than this. It is vital to have a strong middle leadership team who are empowered to try new ideas, and then they must support others in real and meaningful ways.*

The problem before had been that teachers and pastoral staff felt disempowered—learning that if they put their heads above the parapet, those heads would get shot off. It was a whole new ethos to try and persuade the staff that, actually, their ideas were welcomed, supported, and genuinely would impact what happened in the college. Teaching subjects were joined into groups under heads of department who could guide and support their teams.

However, for this to work, the middle leaders clearly needed training.

I sent an email to an inspector friend who planned to come in to look at the maths and science department. I said in the email that "there are clearly issues, and the department is failing." This was a stupid mistake. I had made a swift judgement which belied the hard work some were doing in the team, and when I carelessly forwarded an email with my previous comment in the email trail, I faced some strong words from the deputy in the department. She was right to challenge me, and it did her credit to stand up to me. I learned an important lesson about thinking carefully about how to phrase things and not making snap judgements on the spur of the moment.

"However, am I supposed to tell someone they need to focus on new approaches to teaching? They've been doing it that way for years," one of the new heads of department complained. So, we launched a series of training sessions on leadership and management, highlighting the difference between the two and how to cope with a wide variety of situations.

*Management involves controlling a group to achieve a goal, whereas leadership is about influencing and motivating others while building enthusiasm to share in a vision with you. To pull together as a team, you need effective leadership, and it must be reflected throughout the school.*

Things were moving fast, and my abiding memories of these years became examples of just how much the staff were prepared to listen and take ownership. Many of them realised just how wrong things were at the college, and they had the goodwill and determination to help me bring about change.

Having looked at school structures and teaching, we also had to ensure our students were being listened to and encouraged to engage more fully in the life of the school. Young people also needed to be at the heart of this whole process, so student councils were set up. These groups regularly met with staff, with minutes posted on noticeboards and also emailed out to the student body.

Slowly, the students started to read these emails, as there were now things to see on them. Every week, I would send out information about what was happening in the UK. I would also tell them about English customs we had, from Gunpowder Night to Remembrance Day.

Many had no idea about the rather macabre meaning of Bonfire Night on November 5$^{th}$. It remembers the day Guy Fawkes tried to blow up the king and Parliament in 1605. The plot was foiled, and since then, people in the UK have celebrated with fireworks and burning an effigy of Guy Fawkes on a bonfire.

One student came up to me and said, "Jonathan, why are they singing 'Ding Dong the Witch Is Dead' on TV after the death of one of your great leaders?"

I had to explain that this attempt to make the song "top of the pops" after Margaret Thatcher had died was because opinions about her were polarised—with some vehemently in favour of what she did, and others blaming her for the mass closure of mines and steel plants. Although this behaviour was inexplicable to some of our students, I was able to make the point about us living in a democracy, with everyone holding a right to share their opinions. I shared how some had done this by attending what became a "ceremonial funeral" with pomp and ceremony in London, while others chose to protest at what they saw as her legacy.

I also made a point of visiting the boarding houses to meet staff and pupils and experience life at the college from all angles, while working hard to improve conditions all round with the strong support of the principal.

My time at the school was a key lesson in how *strong leadership must involve and support students and staff alike.*

*Students must feel part of an institution and actively engaged in activities, with their voice taken seriously. Staff need proper training and respect, and leaders need to carry a critical mass with them to achieve change.*

It was because of the support of students and staff alike that the school really started to move forward. International student numbers were rising, since the college had been taken over by a company with private equity, and investment flooded in with new buildings and facilities. The issue of money, financial targets, and key performance indicators was the order of the day and what investors were most interested in.

*In these situations, it is more important than ever to keep faith with students and staff and stand firm on the principles that guide you. It is vital to have a strong sense of what is right and what is in the best interests of the school.*

Meanwhile, I had embarked on a wide series of international trips to meet overseas agents and parents, and raise the profile of the college. I was astonished by my first visits to China to discover the enormous size of new cities I had never heard of before.

Today, China is an amazing growing market with steadily growing demand to attend UK universities. It certainly helps that most of the world's top twenty universities are in the UK or USA. If parents cannot get their children into a top Chinese university, many feel that they need their children to attend a prestigious one in the UK or USA so they do not lose face. Sadly, this also means many students applying who may simply not be up to the mark. They may have weak English or academic abilities, but their parents want them to go to Oxbridge! Aspiration must be matched to reality.

There is also often a feeling that you can cram knowledge, as often happens overseas, and that A-levels can be done in one year with top grades to go to a top university, often with less than strong English. Of course, it just doesn't happen like that. Still, some schools will take the money to put students on one-year Advanced-level courses to go to a top university, even though it seldom works without very careful vetting of students. Yet these large numbers of Chinese students all want to go to a school with no Chinese students in it—a near impossibility today!

I also travelled extensively to Vietnam, where it did amuse me to talk about private education under portraits of Marx and Lenin, and then to Malaysia, Thailand, Singapore, Hong Kong, Indonesia, Burma and a wide range of European countries. These visits certainly raised the profile of our school, and it was a pleasure to help so many people overseas understand UK education, whether or not they ultimately came to the UK.

"So, what exactly must I do to get into a top UK university?" was a question I was asked constantly as I travelled abroad to visit parents and educational agents. I enjoyed speaking to groups to explain all about this, and these visits were great to help boost UK education overseas. Almost all our students now came from over eighty-five different nationalities, and we had eighteen different offices all over the world from which to recruit and support students ready for their journey to the UK.

As an aside from the educational component, the trips were also a real experience for me! I found I could cope with the change of diet in almost all the places I visited, except China. I loved Chinese food in the UK, but of course it's nothing like "real" Chinese. Our Chinese food is generally based on Cantonese (Hong Kong) food, but with a Western twist. However, genuine Chinese food was not a delicacy I was always able to fully appreciate. It gave me a real insight into how international students in the UK sometimes need food from home which they are familiar with.

The staff in our offices in China knew me well. As soon as they saw me, they would say, "Jonathan, I know just what you need," and would rush me off to the local Starbucks or Pizza Hut to fill me with what they thought I needed. They were incredibly kind, and although I wouldn't go to these places much in the UK, they were certainly a welcome input of Western food when I was hot and tired! The rest of the time, of course, the local dignitaries I met wanted to showcase their local cuisine, so I had to smile warmly and get on with it.

The main purpose of the trips was to train overseas staff so they could sell the school places wisely. Ambition and determination showed in both parents and students, but top university places couldn't be bought. Students can't go to Oxford, Yale, or Oxford just because their parents want them to. Managing expectations was a major part of my job.

So, did it all go as smoothly as some of this sounds? Well, of course it didn't! Having set up structures, it was vital to demonstrate that they would be used.

Pupil attendance when I came to the college had been low, and it was clearly stated that students with under 80 percent attendance and low or failing grades on regular assessments would not be entered for exams, as they had not attended enough lessons to be properly prepared for them. I also read all the comments teachers made on reports and checked them against attendance levels. Regular warnings were sent out, but they were clearly not believed by students or staff.

Everyone had to know that the college stood for high standards, and that what we said really did mean something. To help initiate a change, I then shocked everyone by removing students from exam entry who had poor attendance. Many of the staff were horrified and complained.

"But you said on their last three reports they were poorly prepared for their exams, rarely attend lessons, and put very little effort into their work," I countered.

More shock was shown over the fact that I had actually read all the reports and knew what was in them. Long queues of students formed outside my office, and I discussed future plans with shocked students about how they could get to their chosen universities.

Attendance levels rapidly went through the roof, and teaching and learning was given a major boost in the arm. Compassion was exerted in cases where there was due cause, and others had to delay their exam entry plans until they were ready.

The rest of the senior team rapidly headed back to their offices and left me to face the music. I can understand this; I was setting a fast-paced and ambitious agenda, and others did not want to be associated with failure. However, what was certain was that I had every intention of turning the college into something to be proud of.

One of my most moving moments in education happened at this time in the college. I was going downstairs in the lift, which I shared with an African student and his friend. He was the grandson of a major African opposition leader and had seen awful experiences back in his home country. He had faced war and persecution and had terrible memories from the past, but he was determined to put it behind him and succeed in the UK. He turned to me at the height of a period of change, when I was firmly on my own in driving through a change agenda, and said, "I can see what you are doing here for the students and the college, and I just wanted to say thank you." This was a great confirmation from a young man I had much respect for that we were on the right path and really making a difference for our students.

*Giving young people as many chances as you can to express their opinions and feelings is vital—whether it's through tick cards, meetings, questionnaires, or focus groups. All of this has a key part to play.*

We also took care to use confidential online questions to allow students to explore and comment on their mental health and coping strategies. *Many people are crying out for an opportunity to flag up the fact that they are simply not alright. It's an important challenge to ask any school or institution how they allow people to express their feelings when they clearly want or need to.*

Closely linked to well-being was the system of recording attendance. When I arrived, this was clearly broken; but with promises from the IT team, it was supposed to improve rapidly.

Sadly, as with many IT projects, this didn't happen, and the bedrock of keeping students safe and cared for was not fit for purpose. So, I sat down with the IT team and designed a system based around the UK government policy of "Every

Child Matters." It would keep records from teaching and boarding staff in order to see at a glance what was happening with each student. Concerns at night would be swiftly visible to staff the next day in school or to changing shifts in the boarding house.

This was an excellent system in linking our care for students into a comprehensive package. We had a system to match the best, and suddenly our care improved extremely rapidly. Students were registered every lesson, and we could track attendance records in detail and per subject. Those whose levels fell below a certain point were flagged up for fast action.

The parents were paying a large sum in fees, and I was determined they would have value for money. But the students had never had their attendance monitored this closely. For those used to paying their way out of issues or to improve their grades, it came as a shock that they were expected to work and attend classes. Results continued to improve, as did the number of Russell Group university placements. It was rewarding to see so many young people being supported into success and making their parents proud.

Finally, the school in Oxford had the call. After I had worked there for only eighteen months, the inspectors announced they were coming!

Independent schools in the UK are inspected by the Independent Schools Inspectorate (ISI) on behalf of the Office for Standards in Education (OFSTED)—which inspects mainly state schools. They have a very different approach which sits better with the independent sector in general. They judge a school against its aims and how well that institution fulfils them…so one of my first tasks had been to alter the college's general and subjective aims with ones that were clear, quantifiable and could be proved. The college now aimed to fulfil a student's potential and prepare them for their future role as a global citizen. This goal was far more realistic than the lofty phrases about excellence, was able to be evidenced and was far more achievable.

The ISI is very tight on safeguarding issues and meticulous in screening records and ensuring tight organisation and compliance. We knew the college had made excellent progress in just eighteen months—largely as a result of treating staff well and making a real effort to get them on board and working as a team. However, what we knew was not necessarily what the ISI would find, so we had a tough job to make sure that all our hard work was visible and highlighted.

*It is vital for leaders in an inspection to gather and record data to provide evidence of the effectiveness of their work. It's helpful to keep records in an accessible folder so you can flip to key evidence simply and easily. Most evidence will of course be collected from staff and students to see if what you claim stands up in the real world, but clear evidence can easily challenge any false assumptions made.*

I kept clear examples of everything we said we were doing. It was invaluable.

The inspection was still a drain on all concerned. Staff worried about being observed, and the boarding staff were very nervous. We had prepared them all well, so they knew what to expect; but that didn't stop them from worrying.

However, we had nothing to fear. We had transformed from a school that I was convinced the Department for Education would shut down if they visited, to what we were on the day of inspection. We had moved mountains. *It just goes to show that if you have staff coming along with you, school improvement can happen far faster than you think.* All the evidence hinted it would take years to turn a school around, but we had shown it could be done in eighteen months.

The inspectors graded the school as "good" in all areas except one. That area was "leadership," where we were described as "outstanding."

## Strategies for turning round a failing school

- **Understand that change does not come about from one person; it comes from teams.** Finding people who will help you and training them up to support what you are doing is essential. You must possess a critical mass of staff and students supporting you to really make excellent progress.

- **Train and support middle leaders**. These are the powerhouses of a school or organisation. They will drive change and pull their colleagues on board, but they do need effective training and support to do it. Always go for the very best training, as it really will make a difference.

- **Do not be fazed when other senior staff run for the hills!** Sometimes you must be a lone voice, and it's crucial that you have experienced peers outside your school or organisation to bounce ideas off. You need to be self-reflective and prepared to test your ideas against others; if they hold water, stick to your guns. Leadership can be a lonely place.

- **Benchmark progress effectively**. Use effective qualitative and quantitative research to work out how well you are really doing. There are plenty of systems out there to help you, with statistical evidence behind them for fair comparisons. Measuring progress doesn't depend on gossip, meaningless surveys, or intuition, but is based in hard facts.

- **Use focus groups and surveys**. This data gives people with any concerns, including mental health ones, every opportunity to express their worries and concerns. You can learn a lot from these voices.

# Chapter 6
# Moving to Excellence
# and Beyond

*By a complete stroke of luck, the inspection landed in the*
*middle of our university fair…*

I had fully intended to stay at my college in Oxford to oversee
and embed more of the changes we had made. I did not feel
ready to move. However, the strong success at the college had
been widely noted, and I was headhunted to become the new
principal at Chatsdean School in Canterbury—which was
situated in a series of beautiful period houses in the city.

I had been warned that the managing director had
considered closing the school as it only had just over two
hundred students and lacked the cachet of being in a city like
Oxford. However, this seemed like a great opportunity to
work with others and be in sole charge of an exciting
international school, so I accepted the position. I was fully
aware of what needed to be done, and although Chatsdean
School had past issues with inspections, I knew we could fast-
track its success if I pulled together with staff and students to
make that happen.

A former nursing hostel provided student accommodation, and as I arrived, students were being fed in a tent in an increasingly muddy garden while the new refectory was being built. The school's most famous alumni was a well-known international terrorist from the 1970s—a fact pointedly omitted from any of the school literature and prospectus.

As I have shared in previous chapters, schools in the UK attract large numbers of international students who are extremely keen to get into world-ranked universities and want to be prepared to enter them. The English educational system has an outstanding reputation overseas. In fact, there are more British schools being opened around the world than those of any other nationality. The top world universities are dominated by UK and American institutions, and UK universities are particularly popular as they can be a lot cheaper than some top US places of study.

The school had large numbers of part-time staff and the front of the building was jam-packed with cars, which made it look extremely unattractive. However, new private equity partners were rapidly increasing facilities, buying new property on the New Dover Road for accommodation, and increasing numbers of classrooms. It was an exciting time to lead.

As the new refectory was being built, students were forced to cope with being fed in the makeshift dining room which was outside in a tent with a muddy floor. I don't know how they managed with it for so long. It was awful! *But despite circumstances, you must keep going and keep smiling.*

While there, I heard several interesting stories from the past, including safes appearing half way down the road and people sleeping in cars, no doubt part of the urban myth that surrounds schools…All this, however, was in the past, and a new day was dawning.

I discovered a mixture of staff, with some very good teachers and others who just needed ongoing support to keep improving. I was fortunate in having an excellent and experienced deputy head, who I really saw eye to eye with and enjoyed working with. Policies were reviewed and updated, and new discipline and attendance systems introduced.

As at Oxford, we had a clear focus on whole-staff training. We involved strong staff as well as external providers in delivering it. A great effort was made to train middle leaders, set up training for new staff in order to outline expectations. We also hosted newly qualified teachers to ensure they were trained for excellence in the classroom.

In the early stages of school or institutional improvement, as was done in Oxford, *you just have to set out your stall as to what is acceptable and what needs to happen. Clarity of thought and vision is essential so that expectations are very clear.*

One of the first things I did was to get a doorstop and wedge my door open. Staff walked past every day and could see me working, and they knew they were welcome to say hello. The new open-door policy flourished. Students also called by, and just the action of smiling or saying something to them made an enormous shift in the school.

"Are you sure I can come in?" one member of staff asked tentatively as she put her head around the door. "I've never been in the principal's study before and wanted to know what it looks like! Is it really true we can drop by and ask you anything?" She seemed delighted with the new approach.

*No matter how busy you are, it's a key principle of leadership to make yourself available to others. Most staff won't come and see you, but knowing that they can is a great morale booster.*

Staff were also consulted about the new mission statement for the school, and we always aimed to help them be a part of it all.

As I have stated, laying down expectations from the top, although important, was certainly not a long-term strategy. Instead, we needed to help staff become actively engaged in their own training and able to offer real input into it. We set up choices of sessions to attend and canvassed staff opinions. We appointed someone in charge of teaching and learning and set up "trios" where staff were given time in the school day to sit and talk in groups of three about teaching, as they planned ways to introduce new ideas to their lessons. This gave them a sense of accountability to each other but also promoted a focus on strengths and weaknesses. They could learn from each other how to improve.

To broaden this approach further, we set up "teach meets." These were evening sessions where each staff member would be given a nice meal and then speak for ten to fifteen minutes about something they had tried in the classroom. This was great fun and promoted discussion all over the school teachers shared ideas in a supportive, pleasant, and non-threatening format, and a great deal was learned from all involved—including new strategies for starting lessons, instilling learning, and ending lessons.

These soon developed into "lead meets" where staff from other schools came to join in; we discussed ideas and strategies for middle leaders to drive improvement. Staff presented on how to give positive feedback to other teachers, how to deal with difficult staff, and how to track progress in effective and easy ways. Staff were fully involved and led these sessions, which gave them a real sense of ownership. They then fed back on new systems we were developing and how to use them, and their input was always valued and appreciated. Staff had the chance to talk about what they felt strongly about, following their own agendas to improve. This approach allowed them to experiment with their teaching and encouraged them to fly. Mistakes were not to be frowned upon but were seen as learning points on a journey.

This kind of involvement of staff in their own training is the mark of an excellent school. We had large numbers of training schemes running from newly qualified teachers (NQTs) to new staff, in-house training to trios. It soon extended into university research and projects on teaching and learning, linked with our two local universities. It also gave teachers the opportunity to work towards a higher degree while working with us.

All of this really did make us a school for tomorrow. We took seriously work-life balance, supporting staff with creating classroom displays, and helping them devise ways to manageably mark student work while still retaining time for their families.

Records of training were kept online with individual staff accounts, and electronic appraisal systems insisted on sign-off from both parties at each stage. This ensured a positive focus for appraisal and the setting of targets that were fair and reasonable, which helped staff move on.

We opened a new accommodation block, and I invited a well-known senior Anglican bishop to open it. Coincidentally he had also married Jackie and I many years back in Bromley, so it was great to see him again! He made an impassioned speech referencing St Lawrence—a local saint.

He spoke about how St Lawrence was called in by the Romans who demanded from him all the riches of the church. St Lawrence duly rounded up all the local poor, dispossessed, and those in need and presented them to the Romans. "These are the riches of the church," he said. And then he was promptly executed.

This was a story which stayed with me and resonated later in life. I often retold the story to our students, many from wealthy areas all over the world, stressing that *no matter what you go through, people are more important than money or riches.*

*This is a key leadership principle to drive you—valuing people over financial targets and money. Remember what you first came into teaching for and hold firm to it.*

I had amazing times working with the people at Canterbury and other schools. Once again, I became impacted on why it was so important to put people first and encourage young people to speak their minds and be strong. I knew this would help them in the years ahead.

As for me, I was to spend over thirty years encouraging and helping young people, yet I could still be hurt by poor governance and unkind accusations in the future. These experiences taught me that *you must hold fast to your core beliefs and know that if you do your best by others and believe in helping and supporting them, then when things don't work out, you know you have stayed true to your values. This sense of values and sticking to them is so vital to anyone in education and one of the best things we can teach each other.*

But once again, the smooth sailing would not last forever. It all began with a simple clerical error.

"Jonathan, I've made a mistake in transcribing a few of the final marks, and we need to alter them," one of my exam's officers told me. It seemed like a fairly straightforward error that anyone could make. He had simply miscopied a few numbers when transferring data from one sheet to another.

"Do you have any issue with this?" I asked my deputy who oversaw the problem.

"It's fine, Jonathan," he replied, "a simple error—easy to make."

So, we made the changes, which had limited impact on student grades for the course, and we ensured they were fully accurate and as intended. We shared information with two other schools, and suddenly I was accosted by accusations of cheating.

"If there is any suggestion of impropriety," I replied, "I have to refer this directly back to moderators and markers to ensure everything is completely above board." I had no issue with this, as I had been assured it was a simple mistake. I replied to the other schools, "The moderators have signed off on the changes as being accurate and what was intended, so it's all fine and proved as a simple error."

The other schools were extremely rude and ill-tempered about it, but it's really not acceptable to make a big discipline issue over a simple mistake with very limited consequences. I then put the issue to one side and forgot about it.

A week later, a worried deputy head put his head round the door.

"Jonathan, there's something you need to see here," he said. He proceeded to show me the initial results from one of the other schools, against their final grades. There seemed to be a number of major discrepancies which we couldn't readily understand. "What on earth is going on with these marks?" I asked. The marks seemed to have been altered upwards with no indication as to why this was done.

My deputy questioned a little more over email, and in one email was casually told that the head teacher had asked for the alterations to be made. He soon made the obvious link, "The exam grades have been altered to meet the offers made by several top Russell Group universities." We were completely shocked and horrified that this was a possibility. School leaders were changing grades to make themselves look better to outsiders.

We launched further inquiries and asked for a full investigation to take place. The results were conclusive.

"Jonathan," I was told, "there's no reason for the other school's marks to be altered, apart from making a certain number of students meet the standards of their university offers."

It was awful. I had never in my whole career experienced such flagrant cheating to try and improve a school's overall results. I was vocal in expressing my disgust, as was my deputy. The school board was involved from the relevant school, and it finally resulted in the head teacher leaving his post. I was relieved to see the outcome, but it did show just what can happen if due diligence is not followed and meticulous attention to detail gets lost. *It's crucial that mistakes with data be avoided, and fixed immediately if they occur. Leaders must be on the front foot to ensure everything remains fully above board.*

At this point, student numbers at Chatsdean School were rising, and we had soon more than doubled in size. New accommodation blocks opened, and unsuitable ones closed. But some students resided a good distance from the school, which was highly undesirable. While we provided a bus every day for them, each year it got harder to hear and address so many complaints, particularly on arrival at the school.

"What do you mean, where my son lives is going to be *two miles away from the* school?" asked an angry parent. "If you don't put him in better accommodation, we are going home!"

Fortunately, no one did actually turn round and go home, but to be fair, they were justified in their emotions. I hated having accommodation blocks so far away. Offering a bus service for students didn't fully soften the blow. It was really hard having to defend the indefensible.

Our oldest accommodation block was also very shabby, and the wet rooms installed very unpopular. Someone had thought wet rooms were a great idea without checking more about their clientele, who hated them! The German agents wouldn't even let any of their students live there. After much persuasion with our equity partners, we finally had all the accommodation refurbished and got rid of unpopular buildings, which was a great relief. We could now be proud of everything we offered, knowing it had facilities and large ensuite bedrooms for sixth-formers. We kept a small number of double rooms, as there were always some students who preferred these, but the quality of our accommodation was hard to beat for many UK schools.

*The leadership lessons from this are clear. Always listen to your core customers before making changes. What you think is good, they may not. Then always have in mind what provision is acceptable and what isn't. If you don't get this right, you'll have to spend years defending it until the time comes when you're finally able to replace it.*

From the start, I made sure we had an outstanding head of boarding and welfare, who built up a powerful team of supervisors. The market rate of pay for welfare and caring staff is clearly unjust and it was always difficult on the rate of pay we offered to keep attracting them, but somehow, we managed. In spite of the pressure, Kathryn always smiled at me, and her office was a safe haven where I could go and relax and let off steam! She always spoke her mind and was usually right.

Structures were clear and supportive, and we put many boarding staff through training to improve their prospects and skill sets. With tight IT systems, we were able to monitor where students were and provide substantial support. Attendance was driven to new highs, and prizes for high attendance were regularly given. So many were achieving 100 percent attendance; we had a raffle among these top students to decide who got the prize! I lived opposite the school and regularly visited boarding houses to check that students and staff were happy and all was going to plan. We had some great staff, and I took pleasure in seeing how well they cared for their students.

We certainly had moments with some students who, newly released from parental supervision, kept us really on our toes. But the head of boarding was never afraid to hold everyone to account, including me, as she pushed for strong and excellent practice in all areas. My son, Alex, who stayed with me midweek and went to school in Canterbury, came back home with me at weekends. However, he was sometimes left without me as I was called away overseas, but my confidence in the system was such that when I had to leave Canterbury, I often put him in the boarding house. I had no difficulty entrusting him to the watchful eyes of our staff. He viewed it as something of a 'holiday' and enjoyed what was to him the somewhat alien world of school boarding!

*We all need this accountability in leadership positions. We need to actively seek out those who will speak honestly and truthfully. Many will simply tell you what you want to hear, and you must be firmly in touch with those who see things as they really are.*

Alex brought much fun and memories. The day he got a detention, he came back and looked at me, full of rather weak excuses. Finally, he dutifully slunk off to his room after sadly telling me, "You can't put icing on a burnt cake." Through living in Canterbury, he had the opportunity to play rugby for the first time which he thought was great! After his first match he came back to tell me, "Dad, you know rugby is a very violent game…but strangely enjoyable!" To top off the drama, one day I had a visit to my school office of a rather concerned neighbour: "Mr Ullmer, I just thought I had to come over and tell you there is a strange wailing sound

124

coming from the elevator." I swiftly got back to my apartment to discover Alex had got stuck in the lift and had been there for over two hours. I had to call the fire brigade out, who were all over the local road as they planned how to release him and finally got him out.

Meanwhile, Canterbury came out in a national survey as the safest city in the UK, and we marketed the school on the quality of its pastoral care and academic success. Canterbury was the seat of English learning, with a statue of Chaucer in the High Street. Unlike many international schools that focused on maths, sciences, and business, we had thriving provision with drama, art, and humanities. And with our offering of the International Baccalaureate (IB), we had effective provision for an increasingly wide range of students.

*Trying to foster a sense of identity and loyalty within the student body is difficult if they only stay with you for a year.* We were therefore keen to promote longer stays to create a stronger sense of "belonging."

The IB program was a two-year course that encouraged student leadership skills and independent working, while retaining a focus on serving others. This was ideal for our culture. Students had to take science, languages, and a range of subjects. We also offered up to twenty-six native languages—an unheard-of number—and almost all of our students taking IB obtained the dual-language certificate. Students taking the IB course inevitably ended up as mature, well-rounded individuals who had taken a wide range of subjects and were well prepared for university life. Their extended essays and focus on independent learning prepared them well for the future. Many came back later and said how much of a boost the IB program had offered to their integration into university.

It was often hard to recruit students to the IB course, however, as many sales staff and agents only had experience with A-levels. I had to train them as to how different and useful the IB was. Slowly, numbers increased, and we had a strong and viable cohort. These students added colour and vibrancy to the school, and their depth of maturity—which the IB fosters—was a real asset.

Increasing numbers of students also came to us for their exams at age sixteen, and our provision for students from ages fourteen and fifteen steadily grew. This gave students a length of stay at the school of at least four years, which allowed for greater consistency in the student body and encouraged even more of a "collegiate feel" in the buildings.

*This sense of "belonging" is something leaders need to foster and encourage—helping students feel part of a community where they are cared for and listened to, and in which they are given a great education.*

Fortunately, thousands of students did really well and never have a single problem. However, it's always the exceptions that stick in your mind!

"Now what exactly are you doing here?" I asked a group of students who had discovered the joys of the local pub. They were sitting and enjoying an all-day breakfast instead of going to lessons.

"But we *like* this," they replied, "and it's a very English thing to do."

We soon had senior staff patrolling the pub at the end of the road, and the all-day breakfasts stopped. We really had to keep on our toes!

Sex education was also very limited at home for some of our more sheltered students, with one believing it was done through a person's belly button. We had to act "*in loco parentis*" for our students and encourage them to say "no" while focusing on their studies.

Some were not used to suddenly being released from strong parental structures at home. It was vital we kept as tight a reign on these students as possible. I remember one young lady sneaking off to the pub with a friend. She got so drunk we had to call an ambulance. We needed to stay on high alert in listening to what was being said in the boarding houses; then we could proactively forestall students from doing anything daft.

One group of students was rude to some local youths. They were chased all the way back to their boarding house, which certainly taught them a lesson. We then acted fast in putting up new gates to prevent any entry onto the main site without key-swipe access. This minimised the risk of any unauthorised person coming into the school.

However, as students stayed for longer, it gave time for their commitment to the school to grow. They were able to benefit from the many leadership awards we offered instead of packing their experience into one year, as the foundation course students had to do before going to university.

It was about this time I celebrated my fiftieth birthday and hired a small arty venue full of atmosphere to celebrate. I invited people from across my career over the years as well as personal friends, and two former students, David and Terry attended. I remember Terry telling people there I was the best teacher he had ever had and it was great being able to tell people there was one friend here from every one of the twenty-one years I had lived in Westcliff. *Moments to stop and celebrate have to be made in life—we are often so busy we forget to stop and thank people and to share celebrations with others. As leaders we must make time for this and allow others to share in success as well as challenges.*

Meanwhile as numbers grew at school, so did the quality of teaching and pastoral care and its sense of being a welcoming home from home. There is no substitute for where a person grows up, but we were determined to give students every chance to feel happy and supported. Boarding staff and teachers were united in doing their very best to achieve this. I always made a point of eating in the school canteen to show students their food was good enough for all of us, and often brought my son, Alex, with me. I lose track of the times he felt awkward and embarrassed as all teenagers often do with their parents, as I walked among the students eating and asked them about their day and listened to their concerns and issues.

As part of the process of change, we did have to re-contract staff to update their conditions, and from time to time we had to say goodbye to people. As a key leadership principle, I always made sure to brief my senior team on the ethics of this. *It is vital to remain open, transparent, fair, and decent over any redundancy or removal of staff. Staff deserve every opportunity to improve, and we would focus on training and support for anyone who was finding things difficult, with the aim of bringing about better teaching or pastoral experience.*

Lesley was an outstanding teacher who was appointed to focus on staff who were struggling. She would build relationships with them, observe lessons, and give feedback to help them improve their teaching. This had nothing to do with any discipline system; she was purely there to support and help staff.

Richard was a teacher who had come from another independent school and was used to teaching from the front and in a very traditional way. However, with one-on-one help and ideas, he soon adapted to asking students what they had learned. He let them discuss key points to check they had really understood them. His teaching moved to outstanding as he embraced new ideas and worked with his teacher mentor to improve. *Time spent developing people is never wasted.*

The programme of support was generally very successful, and many staff appreciated the time and effort we gave them. Sometimes however, for whatever reason, staff were unable to keep up with the changes needed and had to move on.

One or two staff regularly did badly during lesson observations, with little engagement of the students. Their exam results clearly didn't match the ability of the students they taught.

*Students only get once chance to go through life, and you just must be really clear that they deserve the best we can give them.*

One teacher, caught on camera by a student, was sitting with her feet up on a chair. She was not teaching but instead was just chatting for her lesson. There had been regular complaints about her.

"What do you mean, you don't like my teaching?" she asked after students had reported her. "The students had work to do, so I was relaxing."

She really couldn't see the issue in this, and that this style of teaching had gone out of fashion fifty years ago! In spite of all the efforts to support and train her, it just wasn't working. So, after numerous warnings, she was finally asked to leave.

Our clear focus was always on teaching and learning, and our pupils deserved the best.

One member of staff had to be removed for misogynistic and unpleasant behaviour that clearly has no place in a school, nor does shouting at and abusing students of any age.

I heard another teacher shouting at and belittling a student while I was sitting in my office. She was astonished that she was pulled up for misconduct and disciplined.

We had to be clear about what was and was not acceptable, and that good teaching and mutual respect were demanded of staff. As time passed, a new drive and sense of standards prevailed, with new staff fully supporting what the school was doing. As a result of our efforts, I can remember more than one member of staff, for being so fair and honest with them, coming to thank me after a disciplinary or redundancy process.

*You must stick to your values and principles and impose them fairly and decently. It's a key leadership principle to do whatever you need to correctly, decently, and above board; then it won't come back to bite you later. If you do these things properly and decently, then you should have no trouble sleeping at night.*

The only real unfairness I saw came from a decision to remove a good senior leader because he was associated with a previous regime and spoke clearly in meetings when he didn't agree with significant policies. In this case, things were far from decent and transparent, and he was quite rightly furious about it all. This was an approach I didn't share; it was incompatible with what I stood for. However, this was a clear warning.

*No matter how hard you try, governors can be ill-informed and may not share your vision. This becomes a warning for all of us in leadership to watch our backs and work hard to ensure the vision is shared as much as possible. It's difficult to be caught between those above and below you. Ultimately, you're set for disaster if you don't follow those in a higher position than you, but you can still do your best to sway their mind.*

I often wonder if one such incident was a test of loyalty for me. My manager at the time told me he intended to abolish teaching of the International Baccalaureate at Chatsdean School. I knew it would devastate staff and was a really retrograde step, as the school was defined by its IB, and students taking it were heavily involved in work in the community and helping others.

I did all I could to protect it, but I knew I must ultimately give in to my manager or risk putting myself in a difficult position. If I didn't agree, he would easily appoint someone who did.

I researched and put forward an alternative plan to launch activities across the school to replicate the good of the IB while accepting his decision to abolish it. I had reached the stage of breaking the news to my senior staff, and my manager knew I would support him. He then changed his mind, and the course was reprieved.

*Things don't always have this kind of happy ending. Ultimately, if you don't go with the direction you are paid to go in, remember there are plenty of others who will. So, persuade and share your vision, but in the end, you have to accept the inevitable.*

On another occasion, one of our support staff was arrested by the police out of the blue. He had apparently been downloading images of child pornography. I was horrified by the news and clearly had to go through due process fast. He was immediately suspended pending further action, which we dealt with swiftly. I knew he was facing a prison sentence and would never be allowed to work again with young people, but I had to try and ascertain the impact on the school. He assured me that no images had been taken of students and it had all been outside of the school. We already had pretty robust systems of encouraging pupils to talk, and no mention had been made of him at all. I didn't know how much I could trust what he was saying, but I knew he was a man in a great deal of trouble. So, I handled him decently and fairly, following safeguarding procedures to the letter, pointing out that he would have to be dismissed and face consequences with the police. His life was collapsing around him, so I spoke calmly and kindly, while pointing out the hard action I would be taking. Afterwards he thanked me for being so decent. He said he knew I could have reacted very differently, but I knew it was for the courts to make a final decision, and humanity has to go hand in hand with justice.

We were always meticulous over safeguarding, and I had to insist forcibly on swipe card locks being added to all entrance doors and ensuring the site was as secure as we could make it. Naysayers could always point out that there were still ways around it, and no system is perfect. However, if something happened, I always wanted us to be able to say we had done our very best and made premises as secure as possible. We were meticulous about checks.

*In a position of leadership, it's always crucial to say and feel that you did everything you could. Nothing in life is ever guaranteed, but people are quite rightly angry if they feel things were left undone that could have been fixed, as it can easily be read as a lack of care and attention.*

After all the issues with staff and steadily moving the school forward, we started to experience some real positives. Once you are known for outstanding work, the awards soon start to come. Our efforts paid off in the middle of our hard work, and we were named as international High School of the Year and then highly commended in the independent schools Award of Excellence. We then won the Award of Excellence from the Independent Schools Association and the Times Educational Supplement Boarding Award. We were then shortlisted for three independent school awards in 2017.

It was great for the school to receive these accolades, but we wanted to go even further. We wanted to make sure that these awards reflected a great school experience for every single one of our students.

In the UK, every school says that they have outstanding extra curricula provision, sports, and arts, and are best at everything! So not surprisingly, many agents around the world were sceptical about any claims about activities offered particularly when many of these opportunities were only open to the select few who could win awards and reflect well on their school. We decided to take a completely different approach, determining to ensure that great opportunities were available to all, and committing to being a fully inclusive school. We felt it wasn't fair that the best activities were only offered to the best students.

Instead of talking about how great we were, we produced booklets that listed all the activities and opportunities open to every single student in the school. This proved a powerful tool, showing that we were completely committed to inclusivity. Everyone deserves a chance, and we were clear in holding ourselves publicly to account for everything we did for young people.

We then translated the booklets into major languages to help parents who didn't speak English see exactly what we did. We wrote a strong series of booklets covering all the things parents wanted to talk about, from applying to universities in the UK and USA to how each child was looked after in their boarding house, and what activities they did there with their house parents. More booklets followed on courses we offered, what activities to get involved in to create a powerful CV or university application, how we helped pupils who were ill, and much more. It was great to be able to provide sceptical parents with exact details of what was happening back in England rather than just offering empty words, and our reputation and numbers continued to soar every year.

Our numbers going to top universities continued to grow, as our international students were given great and valuable experiences and became highly sought after. We were also clearly delivering a hidden, and sometimes not so hidden, curriculum of liberalism, tolerance, and democracy—demonstrating how to live in a country without fear or favour. We really were promoting the British way of life, which was often a strong contrast to home. These endeavours would no doubt bear much fruit in the years ahead for the UK and beyond.

One of our greatest successes was our leadership awards which we helped students to obtain. We strongly encouraged every student to see leadership development as starting in youth. We trained them in team working and creative thinking skills, and all the attributes essential to a top UK education. We did this primarily through a series of leadership awards with a wide range of activities and challenges they needed to complete. We offered language, maths, and music leadership along with the International Award, Young Enterprise Award, and many more. Every student was encouraged to complete at least one of these alongside whole-school leadership activity days, with the option of taking an online university course.

We also created a special pathway for students wanting to go to university to study medicine, engineering, architecture, law, banking, business, and more. This gave students the chance to really focus on skills and activities that would boost their chances of acceptance to these university courses. We used Olympiads in chemistry, physics, and biology; the *Young Enterprise Journal*; and visits to the London Metal

Exchange to name but a few, all overseen in detail by our excellent head of higher education at the school.

All these pathways were published for all parents and students to see, so everyone had the chance of participating in them. This also meant we could be held to account for ensuring that the offerings were fully in place. These extra activities and pathways formed part of the Chatsdean School Baccalaureate, which we were in the process of validating with a local university towards the end of my time at the school.

## Excellent in all areas

When we faced our next inspection, we were more than ready. By a complete stroke of luck, it happened to fall in the week when we held our university fair with nearly eighty universities attending. It was a stunning demonstration of the position we had reached when we could attract universities from LSE to Oxford, Durham to Manchester, UCL to Kings— all coming to spend the day talking to students. I was able to update them on what we were doing at the school. Meanwhile the inspectors were rigorous, and we had to keep on the ball in making sure they were aware of everything we were doing. The booklets helped a lot, as inspectors could readily see what the school was about.

The only main issue we faced was the foundation course, as it was not an internationally recognised qualification, and they were tempted to only look at our Advanced (A)-level and International Baccalaureate results. I sat the inspector down to talk.

"Is there a reason why you aren't taking into account our foundation course in your assessment of academic achievement?" I asked.

"Well, it's not a recognised Advanced-level course that students in other schools take," he replied.

I then pushed him quite hard.

"So, you're *discriminating* against our international students because they don't take the same exams as English students? The course is recognised for university entrance, and I have over eighty universities sitting in the sports hall talking to our students. Those universities are prepared to offer these students places based on their results from this exam. You can go down the road and ask them about it yourself."

Of course, discrimination is such a loaded word; it soon had the lead inspector beating a track to my door. I pointed out the same thing to him, and my case was made. It was impossible to ignore the positive comments of top universities from around the world who were actually sitting in the school, talking to our students.

*It just goes to show how leaders must stand up to assumptions made by others and not take things lying down.* Our top priority was to our students and staff, and we owed them to ensure that their hard work was presented in the very best way possible.

We completed the inspection and were rated as "excellent" in every single area. It was a stunning achievement for a former small tutorial college that had now become a strong and successful school, while meeting our aims of preparing students to be global citizens.

While I was at Canterbury, in 2014, I also became an independent (private) school inspector. I enjoyed visiting other schools to see what they were doing, interviewing staff, and going over school details to discover what was great about each school.

The Independent School's Inspectorate (ISI) grades schools on how they match up to their aims (so make these manageable!), and it is far more sympathetic to what schools are trying to achieve. By contrast, Ofsted (the predominantly state school inspectorate) members have sometimes made up their minds before they even arrive about how good they think a school is, and their obsession with data can be taken to extremes. As I write, a popular head teacher in Kent has just committed suicide following a grossly unfair judgement of "inadequate" for the school she worked so hard for. Government bodies such as Ofsted and the Teachers Regulatory Agency have much to answer for in cases where they have clearly abused hard-working members of staff. It's no wonder there is such a shortage of teachers in the UK.

The inspection process really confirmed for me just how far behind state schools many private schools are. I remember asking one pupil at a school, "So what do you think you have to do to improve your work?" and "What is your target grade?"

They often seemed to have little idea, and I was met with platitudes like, "I need to work harder."

It was clear that research showing how students needed to have clear targets for improvement just hadn't permeated many private schools. Markings could often be merely "well done," a mark out of ten, or "I really enjoyed reading about this," which were often a complete waste of effort. I found that American schools are also rather wanting in this respect. Teaching and learning, and also marking, have undergone a transformation in many state schools in the UK.

*Students need to know in their marking what exactly they need to do to improve.*

I am always amused to see government ministers and newspapers laud the private sector. Often, they are out of date, not in touch with the latest educational research, and way behind their state counterparts. There are of course some amazing exceptions, such as the Duke of Kent School in England, which was incredibly innovative in its approach, using research on thinking skills and learning to excellent effect. Students knew what their grades were as well as their target grades, and they had a clear idea of what they needed to do to improve. Many schools, however, don't appear to measure a student's ability against their progress. The results are so good only because students were inherently bright and well-motivated, rather than because of strong teaching.

So, where you do go when, at the other extreme, you have been rated as excellent in all areas? We had new accommodation blocks and common rooms, and excellent university preparation—how could we move further? We couldn't compete with schools with theatres or sports centres, but we had hired a local sports centre for many years when we needed it, which was right on our doorstep, and we now had a drama studio. We were meeting the core needs of our students, with their determination to get to a UK university as their top priority. However, we then negotiated a link with a local high school so we could put talented students through a top-rated local sports academy.

## Call me Jonathan...

One thing I always insisted on was being introduced as "Jonathan." This subverted normal expectations of distance from a principal.

Many of our students had not even known who their school principal was, but I was determined to be seen and heard. Regular communication with students through email, assemblies, and dropping into school boarding houses to chat with students and staff made me a well-known figure, and students were encouraged to speak their minds. This felt similar to doctors doing their "rounds" and checking how everyone was doing! It's also recommended in some consulting models for leaders to do in order to touch base with their staff.

"Would you like a game of table tennis?" one student nervously asked me as I walked into their common room.

"I'd love to," I replied and as the young people relaxed, they told all kinds of stories about their lives.

"We never knew who the headteacher was at our last school," one of them told me. "His office was at the top of one of the buildings, and he never seemed to come down from it."

Many cultures we catered for had quite a background of not speaking out and were expected to absorb knowledge rather than criticise or challenge it, so this was a big thing for them to be taught how to speak out and see their comments and opinions were listened to and welcome.

"Whatever are you cooking? It smells delicious!" I told one student as I walked into their kitchen area.

"It's a local delicacy from home," he explained and went on to show me how everyone in the house was preparing food to eat together to reflect their different cultures. I learned a great deal about them and their home lives, and these interactions soon opened up conversations about how they were finding life at school.

## The importance of student voice

From early days, we did a great deal of work on student voice. We set up card boxes with pre-printed cards including smiley and other faces on to encourage students to say how they felt about their accommodation. We put similar boxes in the dining room and printed comments students made, along with our comments below answering points raised. Students could then see that their comments were being read and acted on.

Another small thing we did was print postcards from boarding house staff, the principal, and vice principal. Often when a residence held a meeting for everyone, we would go round before and after and knock on each student's door just to say "Hi" and ask how they were doing. If they were out, we would leave a card. Students were pleased and quite moved to get a "card" from someone. Often students would drop in at my office and thank me for their "card."

We also had cards to reward students for speaking English around the school instead of their native languages and others as a "thank you" and "well done" for things they may have done around the school. Staff were also able to hand these out.

We knew it worked, as we often saw these pinned up in the students' rooms. Any kind of recognition is always healthy and appreciated, and we were always looking for ways to link with our student body and encourage them!

However, by far the best system we set up was the "Tell Us" button. This appeared prominently on our internet page, as well as around the school. When students clicked on it, it took them to a variety of other buttons tied to different issues. There were buttons for accommodation problems, visa issues, teaching, safeguarding, sports, university applications, and every other issue you could think of. Students just had to click on one of these buttons, and it took them to a form to fill in. Their entries then went by email directly to two people in charge of each area. Our promise was that if they didn't hear back within forty-eight hours, then they could go direct to the principal who would sort it out for them. Not surprisingly, I had very little referred to me. Staff were swift in responding to issues. The best thing was it avoided what I had noticed, which were situations where students said things to their busy teachers, and the issues never got referred on or dealt with. Teachers probably thought it wasn't their area, or in the rush of the day, they simply forgot. We wanted to give students direct access to people at the top who could make things happen. It also provided a great comeback to serial complainers, as the first question I would ask them was, "Have you put your issue on the "Tell Us" button?"

Students soon got the hang of this process. It demonstrated our encouragement of the student voice while also providing a means for students to be heard. They could submit things confidentially of course, but we did warn them that if their comments did not have their names on them, we would not be able to reply personally to them. Some students were initially too scared to put their name on a complaint, but to our delight, this soon waned over time as they became more confident in the school and the principal.

We aimed throughout to shift student experience so they knew they would be listened to and could speak their minds. Alongside student councils and house meetings, all of which had their minutes put up on noticeboards to read, we were determined to be a listening school.

We were soon shortlisted for the Times Educational Supplement Boarding School of the Year for our commitment to student voice, and ended up winning the accolade. We were also shortlisted for UK Independent School of the Year.

*Listening isn't about doing one thing—it's about doing many different things to allow people to comment in whatever way they are comfortable with—in meetings, by anonymous cards, or via "Tell Us" buttons on the internet.* Any way we could find was used, and we started to create generations of young people who were increasingly able to express themselves and grow in confidence.

*There is good research by Prosci stating that people need to hear things five to seven times before they will act on it, and with different learning styles, students may prefer different channels to communicate with. Being listened to makes people feel part of an organisation, like they and their opinions are valued. Any institution that neglects this does so at its peril. We all need engaged workforces and people who feel valued and appreciated.*

It was not surprising that awards kept coming, as our initiatives and practices had really moved us beyond *excellence* compared to other schools at the time. We won awards for outstanding sixth-form provision, the Award of Excellence from the Independent Schools Association, became an accredited international school, and were shortlisted or highly commended for other awards. We were soon running out of space in the entrance hall to fit them all!

At the end of each term, we made a point about having celebrations with drinks and food. These events were popular and gave staff the chance to relax and chat together.

*People who work hard deserve to be thanked. Good leaders never forget to say thank you, as you can't do anything without staff supporting behind you.*

The most surprising award, however, came in 2014. A group of former students and staff from many of the schools I had worked in up till then wrote a range of letters to the UK Cabinet Office. After a long process of sifting and checking, I found myself opening an envelope to a request that invited me to accept the award of the Order of the British Empire. To say it was a shock was an understatement! So, I duly became an MBE.

It was amazing to take my wife and children with me to Buckingham Palace in what was an exciting and moving day. It was like going into toy-town to see soldiers with swords drawn, beefeaters, and Gurkha soldiers—before being presented with the medal which I dedicated to all the students and staff I had been so privileged to work with.

Any kind of recognition for hard work is appreciated, and I had learned this lesson well in my days at Chatsdean School. It was a real pleasure doing it all, and I don't regret one minute of it all.

## Moving to excellence and beyond

- **Encourage staff to control their own training**. You can start to do this when you are confident you have a strong body of staff who are ready to share ideas. When staff can identify areas, they want to improve in and are given time to work with others to do this, the staff are really learning to fly, which is a mark of excellence.

- **Celebrate regularly with all staff.** This isn't about freebies or parties; it's about showing staff you care and value them. A buffet at a local restaurant or in school after the end of term allows staff to relax together after all their hard work. Include all the staff and not just teaching staff; everyone plays a part in making a school successful. You also need to look out for awards you can apply for, which provide another accolade for staff and students. Awards are offered by many bodies including the Times Educational Supplement (private and state schools) or the Independent Schools Association in the UK, and many more overseas. You will find there is always something award-worthy, and it's worth taking your time to write a bid to highlight it. Awards encourage staff and provide independent verification of the great work they are doing.

- **Seek every opportunity to engage**. Use cards with smiley or sad faces, online feedback on intranets, formal surveys, staff bulletins, whole school meetings, comment cards, or focus groups. All of them can be incredibly helpful in engaging with your staff and students and helping them feel part of a community.

- **Be fair, decent, transparent, and honest.** This is particularly important when harsh decisions must be made. People need to know you have thought about them, care, and will do all you can to offer support.

# Chapter 7
# The Importance of Governance

*The call from Kazakhstan…*

As our children embarked on their university journeys, I unexpectedly stumbled upon an opportunity that would alter the course of my career. A position as the head teacher of Hallsworth School in the bustling capital of Kazakhstan caught my attention, although I hadn't actively sought a change at that moment. Yet, as the idea took root in my mind, I couldn't help but wonder. I had developed a deep connection with Kazakh students over the years through my work and visits to the country, even familiarising myself with the school itself. It occurred to me that this could be the perfect final endeavour before my retirement, a chance to make a lasting impact.

Reaching a certain stage in one's professional journey often sparks a desire for something new. After years of facilitating young students' journeys to study in the UK, I felt an urge to settle in a different country and experience first-hand what generations of my own students had done. While my amazing wife, Jackie, couldn't pursue her passion for working as a midwife abroad due to health reasons, she fully supported the notion of us venturing overseas together, with me as a head teacher and her by my side.

Of course, our decision to leave our home in the UK and embark on this ambitious journey surprised not only our children but also our friends. To them, it seemed unfathomable. However, to Jackie and me, it felt like the most natural progression. After all, my career had to come to an end eventually, so why not conclude it with a remarkable and unforgettable experience in helping others? The prospect of embracing a completely different environment in our sixties was undeniably exhilarating and we were also aware the church over there also needed support. We were determined not to fade into retirement quietly; rather, we saw Kazakhstan as a gateway to the next phase of our lives.

To many, our choice was met with confusion and incredulity. Friends and acquaintances bombarded us with questions like, "Where is Kazakhstan?" and "Why on earth are you going there?" However, we knew exactly what had compelled us to consider leaving our comfortable UK existence, journeying around the world, and accepting a position in a relatively unknown country. It was a surprising decision, even for us. I sought a fresh challenge, and this opportunity seemed tailor-made for my expertise. While I anticipated inevitable challenges, given the sometimes outdated methodologies and practices prevalent in UK private and international schools, I reassured myself that the prestige associated with the Hallsworth name would make the transition smoother. Little did I know that those would later become famous last words, but they didn't dampen my excitement for this incredible adventure.

## False starts

The interview process that followed was intriguing. Three candidates, including myself, were invited to stay at Hallsworth UK with our partners. The series of in-depth interviews proceeded as expected, and I navigated them with confidence, challenging notions and showcasing my strengths. A minor setback occurred when the initially advertised salary seemed lower than expected. However, I believed that with goodwill from both parties, that could be resolved. Eventually, at the evening dinner, clearly meant to test our etiquette and conversation skills (!), I was approached privately and informed that I was the clear frontrunner for the role.

The following day involved presentations, during which I faced unexpected scrutiny regarding salary matters, despite it having already been advertised. I wondered if some of the governors hadn't thoroughly read the brief, but I brushed it aside. Soon thereafter, I received the surprising news that my application had not been successful, and I would not be invited to Astana, the Kazakh capital. Although taken aback by this turn of events after the positive reception I had received throughout the process, I understood that the decision ultimately rested with the governors. Thus, I refocused my attention on my work in Canterbury, which was immensely fulfilling.

Time passed, and it became evident that the situation was not as it initially seemed. A call from the agency handling the case offered profuse apologies for the mishandling of the interview process by Hallsworth.

"Look, Jonathan," they asked, "we're really sorry, but we need to apologise for the way the whole interview process was

149

handled with Hallsworth. I've no idea what they were doing, and I quite understand if you don't want to have anything more to do with it. But would you be open to considering the post again?"

"Well," I replied, "it was certainly one of the strangest interviews I've been through. But these things happen, and you know how much I enjoy working with Kazakh students. Would you like me to see the people at Hallsworth again?"

"No," she replied, "I want you to fly out to Astana and meet the Kazakh governors. They are very keen to see you."

Despite the strangeness of it all, I recognised that such circumstances can arise, and my fondness for working with Kazakh students allowed me to respond positively. The agency proposed that I bypass further meetings at Hallsworth and instead fly directly to Astana, where the Kazakh governors, who held firm control over the school's funding and enjoyed close ties with the Kazakh President, were eager to meet me.

As the days went by, I found myself unexpectedly being flown out to Astana, the vibrant capital of Kazakhstan. This journey was meant to introduce me to the school and the influential individuals who were the major funders behind its construction. They held significant positions, close to the Kazakh President, and were the driving force behind this endeavour.

Upon my arrival, I received a warm welcome and had the opportunity to meet the acting head of the school. He made it clear that he fully supported my application and expressed his enthusiasm about having me onboard. I engaged with the staff, listening attentively to their concerns and issues. Their reception was incredibly warm, making me feel like I was already a part of this remarkable place. It was as if I had seamlessly fit into the environment—a natural connection had begun to form.

The next step in the process involved meeting the enigmatic figures who were the silent forces behind the scenes. These individuals had not been present during the interviews I had at Hallsworth but were the investors backing the entire project. They whisked me away to a towering building in the heart of the city. We ascended high into the sky, and it was there that I was introduced to Mr Setimov, an imposing and no-nonsense man who commanded respect. He bypassed the UK representatives in the room, addressing me directly. "I've witnessed the impact of your work here, and I believe you possess the qualities of an exemplary head teacher," he stated firmly. "I require someone with experience and maturity, someone who can effectively manage the school and tolerate no nonsense from staff or distractions from Hallsworth. Will you come and lead this institution for me?" Mr Setimov had a copy of my curriculum vitae before him, translated into Russian, yet he conversed with me fluently in English. Despite his serious demeanour, I could see the determination in his eyes and sensed that he truly meant business. It was at that moment that I envisioned myself working under his command.

Subsequent meetings ensued with the somewhat nervous Hallsworth governors, whom I boldly pressed on my stipulations and requirements while working overseas. *As leaders, it's imperative to recognise our own worth and never undervalue the unique contributions we bring to the table.* The governors appeared intimidated, fearing I might decline their offer, and I could perceive their lack of a backup plan.

After discussing the opportunity with close friends and consulting with Jackie, I made the decision to embrace this new chapter in my life. I became the latest addition to the lineage of Hallsworth Head teachers.

Later on, I discovered some intriguing facts about what had transpired behind the scenes. It seemed that despite the availability of another candidate willing to accept a lower salary than mine, for reasons still unknown to me, they had chosen to send him to the school instead. I couldn't fathom the rationale behind it, but I soon learned that the staff's response to his arrival was less than favourable. Some voiced their disappointment, questioning whether they deserved better. The acting head teacher, who had been horrified to learn earlier that I didn't have the job, even threatened to resign. It became evident that Hallsworth was caught in a state of chaos. On the other hand, the Kazakh governors were insistent upon meeting me after reviewing my CV.

Amidst the apologies from the chair of Hallsworth governors in Kazakhstan, I remained confident in my understanding of the Kazakh people and their aspirations for the school. Years of experience had granted me valuable insight into their preferences. My son, Alex, as always, carried himself with both determination and excitement. When our move finally became a reality, he proudly shared with all his university friends that his parents had "flown the nest." Although I should have acknowledged the warning signs, I firmly believed that this opportunity held tremendous potential. Jackie and I were determined to embark on this incredible adventure, and a few missteps on Hallsworth's part were not going to deter us. Throughout my life, I had always been an optimist, eager to trust in the best and forge ahead.

This approach had occasionally landed me in challenging situations, but I firmly believed that life is meant to be lived to the fullest, taking risks and embracing every opportunity for adventure. Thus, I accepted the position with resolve, ready to throw myself into the incredible experience that awaited me.

## Astana—the adventure begins

Rather than contenting myself with the comforts of my life in the UK, I eagerly prepared myself to immerse in the Kazakh culture. I meticulously reviewed their policies, striving to understand every aspect of the school. I made several visits, gradually familiarising myself with the surroundings, all the while looking forward to the day I would officially begin my tenure. Astana, nestled amidst the vast Kazakh Steppe, provided a breathtaking view from tall buildings, extending for miles in profound emptiness. During winter, temperatures plummeted to a bone-chilling minus 40 degrees, while the summer brought a warm embrace of 30 degrees or higher.

Astana, with its modern marvels of high-rise structures and architectural wonders by the likes of Norman Foster, exuded a futuristic ambiance. The people, once you got to know them, were warm and friendly, carrying within them a rich nomadic heritage. Many families lived together in small apartments, reminiscent of their ancient nomadic lifestyle. However, this way of life had been tragically disrupted by Stalin, as thousands fell victim to the harsh famines caused by the forced collectivisation of lands. Consequently, the Kazakh people harboured mixed feelings towards their Russian neighbours. Despite their close proximity to Russia, they strived to strike a delicate balance between complying with those they relied on and nurturing their own cultural heritage. In a testament to their pride, Kazakh was soon to be mandated in the civil service.

I had encountered a glimpse of their deep-rooted pride during my time in the UK, when one of our Kazakh students tragically died following a road accident. The other Kazakh students displayed incredible loyalty and solidarity, supporting and remaining with the grieving family. The Kazakh funeral traditions touched my heart deeply. Once I relocated to Kazakhstan, I experienced first-hand their caring and people-centric society.

As the head teacher, I was privileged to have my very own driver named Amiel, who, along with his family, prepared a heartfelt dinner for us early on in our stay. We embarked on a journey to select a lamb, an occasion during which prayers were offered before the animal's sacrifice. At the dinner, each one of us was allocated a specific part of the lamb or even its head, paying homage to their revered traditions. It was truly moving to be so closely involved in their lives.

## Breaking down barriers

The school itself bore a modern interpretation of Hallsworth UK, designed in a sprawling quadrangle. I was fascinated to discover that a small corridor had been constructed with special materials, allowing a fire engine to seamlessly drive through in the event of an emergency, sacrificing that portion of the building to reach the centre of the quad. To infuse the institution with a vibrant and engaging atmosphere, I collaborated with the talented director of studies, to implement new displays, incorporate fish tanks, and bring about various other enhancements. These efforts aimed to brighten the learning environment, mirroring the best practices from the UK educational system. Supported by an exceptional senior team, boasting diverse levels of experience, we were all driven by a shared vision and unwavering focus as we moved forward.

During my time in Kazakhstan, Amiel, my dedicated driver, would pick me up from my apartment in the city and drive me to the school. When selecting my apartment, I deliberately chose one with a spacious entertaining area with beautiful views overlooking the river and near the heart of the old town. I knew that regular staff parties and gatherings would be an essential part of my tenure, and I believed in treating the staff with respect, just as we had done in the UK.

Initially, many of the Kazakh staff were hesitant to attend these events, mistakenly thinking that the invitation was only extended to the UK staff. However, as they realised, they were warmly included and welcomed, their hesitation faded away. As Jackie and I opened our lives to them, they reciprocated and became an integral part of our journey. One of the most moving experiences during my time there was attending a traditional Kazakh wedding of one of my staff members. It was great to see rather than one or two speeches on the Western model of weddings, each table stood up to speak and send their love and best wishes to the happy couple. There was also more than one event—the bride and groom marked the leaving of one household with one event, and another event to welcome them into their new one. It was very family orientated and it was not only moving but also a delight to play a part in. We also spent cherished moments with Amiel's family, whether it was on holidays or visits to various places. Amiel introduced us to activities such as skating, watching football and ice hockey, enchanting sleigh journeys, and we enjoyed horse-riding in the mountains of the south. He acted as our translator and guide and was always there to get us out of any tricky situations.

During one memorable occasion on a mountain overlooking stunning lakes, Amiel engaged in a heartfelt conversation with my children, Alex and Philippa. He asked them about their lives at university and their aspirations for the future. In turn, Alex asked Amiel about what he considered to be truly important in life. Amiel replied with great emotion, "It's my family. They provide an essential foundation and support that helps you weather any storm. By investing time in them and embracing strong family values, you won't go far wrong." His speech deeply impressed my children, reminding them of the significance of maintaining strong bonds with family and friends in life's journey. I, too, cherished the powerful role that friends and family played in lifting me during challenging times and supporting me unconditionally along the way.

In addition to the personal connections we developed, there were also numerous diplomatic events to attend. Hallsworth became well-known among local expats and embassies, and we often worked together with other schools, with me eventually serving as the chair of the Confederation of Astana Schools. At the school itself, my role entailed leading the launch of the International Baccalaureate Diploma and ensuring that students had excellent university prospects by aligning with top UK practices in exams, ethos, and academic performance. The majority of the student population consisted of Kazakh and Russian students, with the remaining students being children of teachers, embassy staff, or employees of multinational companies.

To acknowledge the revival of the Kazakh language, which had been suppressed during years of communist rule, we reshaped the curriculum to include Kazakh as a second language. Interestingly, most of our students, including many Kazakhs, were learning the language as their second. I believed it was essential to treat parents with the utmost respect by initiating conversations in Kazakh, then Russian, and finally English. This gesture not only fostered strong relationships but also demonstrated our admiration for their language and culture. The local Kazakh students at the school truly appreciated this approach, and I am forever grateful to the Kazakh staff who patiently taught me the language.

One day, a European student asked me, "Why do I have to learn Kazakh?" I responded, "It's about showing respect to the country we live in. Moreover, it's a fantastic opportunity to learn more about the language spoken in this incredible place. When you return home, think about how many of your friends will be able to say they can speak some Kazakh?" Our exchange ended with smiles exchanged between us.

Our son Alex came over to work for a short spell with the British embassy in Astana, and then for a local non-governmental agency, his blond hair clearly picked him out from all the darker haired Kazakhs. The assumption often made was that he was Russian, and once when walking along the river with a local Kazakh girl, he faced shouts and aggression from other young people, and had an ice cream thrown at his head. It was amusing to look back on, but it did highlight the underlying tensions which within a few years saw riots on the streets of Almaty, the former capital city. All these things had to be factored in, and I worked with the American Embassy to draw up contingency plans in the event of the death of the President, or any unrest in the new capital. *You have a responsibility to always consider the unthinkable as a school leader, and ensure you are ready for it.* Progress was made with excellent local staff, and I insisted on visits to local cultural institutions and the setting up of Kazakh Days to celebrate their culture and language. I closed the whole senior school for a number of days and made all the students go and live in a yurt and experience Kazakh culture. Even the President's son attended, riding his horse, reminding us of the strong Kazakh culture we had nurtured and supported.

## Getting to know the school

However, as my first months at the school passed and I became more familiar with its operations, I discovered significant issues that needed addressing. The school did not align with my initial expectations, and I soon realised that there were problems concerning safeguarding, organisation, and teaching and learning. References had not been thoroughly checked, and the school lacked a clear focus on meeting the academic needs of some students. Data analysis was sporadic and lacked a robust strategic approach. I was determined that for the large sums the Kazakh owners were paying for the school, they deserved to have better value for money.

To address these concerns, I reached out to experts from the UK with extensive experience in both primary and secondary education. They responded to my call and made the journey to Astana.

"I want you to provide the additional support I need to set up an effective coaching and mentoring scheme to support staff and improve teaching in a supportive and non-confrontational way," I briefed them. The aim was to boost teaching skills and give individual help and support to develop middle leadership so there would be effective teaching and monitoring throughout the school. "In the process," I added, "I'd also like you to take a close look at the school as it is now. Then come back several times to measure progress and give me an independent, unbiased view on what is going on here."

The aim was to enhance teaching skills and provide individual help and support for the development of middle leadership, ensuring effective teaching and monitoring throughout the school. Additionally, I invited Rachel Smith, a remarkable leader in primary education, to closely examine the primary school. All the experts concurred with my assessment. Rachel informed me, "Where data is available, it is evident that insufficient progress is being made in English teaching. The school is clearly falling short." The feedback from the other UK advisors echoed this sentiment, urging us to take prompt action.

In my headmaster's report to the governors in June 2018, I talked about some important things we needed to work on at the school. First, there was no central register of staff, and Kazakh staff had not been briefed to keep full records of references and official checks that were needed. We also needed to update our primary school curriculum and how we assessed and reported on students' progress. Our assessment systems were inadequate, with 23-page long reports that made it hard for parents who spoke a different language to understand. Plus, we didn't have accurate data to measure how students were doing or set goals for improvement.

It turned out that our school wasn't aware of some important inspection requirements either. But I wasn't about to let these challenges stop us! We knew we had to improve student learning and progress, especially in English. So, we made major changes to improve performance management, safeguarding and teaching and learning structures.

The issues were indeed serious. One governor promptly turned round and summed it up: "This clearly shows a major failure of governance at the school." The rest of the governors remained silent, and I didn't comment further.


## Taking the bull by the horns...

I was very concerned by these failings and decided it was essential to check my findings against what the experts had found. They confirmed what I had already discovered, that the school was underperforming. All the experts had agreed with my conclusions about the problems at the school, and the senior team was determined to address them. Student learning was not measured, they were not making sufficient progress in English, and there were few structures in place to address this.

To deal with these issues, I led our team in increasing time given to English and key subjects, so that teachers would have more time to teach students who had English as a second language. Those struggling were able to drop subjects to focus on English skills or to spend additional time to work on other subjects. We also increased involvement and extracurricular time and leadership awards markedly to encourage independent learning and the skills needed to succeed. More importantly, having come to these judgements, I asked the experts to return several times to check on the improvements that were being put in place and to comment on how things were now changing at the school.

The experts returned several times, and at each visit, they commented on the speed of improvement, validating our efforts to turn the school around. We were heading for Hallsworth's first inspection as an international school, and it was vital for the Kazakhs that we show the very best of what was possible.

We soon set up sustainable mentoring systems to support staff training. Not only did we provide whole-school training, but we also focused on those teachers who most needed extra help to improve their delivery in the classroom. We also moved towards creating a culture of continuous improvement, mentoring support, and ongoing help for staff. New performance management systems stressed agreed targets and regular reviews, and all training was logged so staff had clear records of all their training experiences. Early results were encouraging, as more staff engaged with the process. We were moving fast towards excellent practice.

I soon launched changes to the house system to make it a pastoral and academic one, rather than simply cheerleading, bringing it in more in line with UK private schools. A new learning technology strategy was put in place, and I moved quickly to achieve accreditation with American diplomas. Soon we had passed all the early stages of membership to the New England Association of Schools and College and the

Council of International Schools, who praised our work highly.

It's surprising just how many international schools are led without clear vision and its vital to have a clear sense of direction. We were determined to offer both US and international qualifications and we clearly aimed to reach the heights as one of the world's top international schools within four years of my arrival at Hallsworth, in spite of the issues I had discovered when I arrived. We widened the curriculum at a stroke by altering the timetable to put all the old after-school activities on after lunch as part of the timetable and lengthened the school day so one hundred percent of students were involved in extracurricular activities.

## Living by values

We soon won a number of international awards and were shortlisted for awards from organisations within the country. We were also shortlisted for a top award from the Times Educational Supplement in the UK. We were well on the way to success.

"I'm exhausted, standing here waiting for the children," one parent mentioned as they stood around in separate groups waiting for children to arrive.

"I know what you mean," I replied, and soon we built a new coffee shop with cakes and drinks and a seating area to make the school entrance hospitable and welcoming.

"Jonathan, you drink far too much coffee," was the response from almost all my senior staff as I encouraged others to sit and chat there…However, the moments I had in a busy day to sit and work at a table with coffee made me available in the same way I had been with my office door open in Canterbury, and I enjoyed the many conversations I had there with parents, pupils and staff alike.

With our strong focus on safeguarding, the head of arts faculty then asked me, "What about the particular needs of music and drama teachers?"

"I think you're spot on," I replied, and we soon designed special leaflets for drama and music teachers, security guards, and parents. All explained simply, backed up with banners in the entrance hall, what they needed to know to ensure students were safe and well-cared-for.

A new whole-staff contract was again making clear our commitment to safeguarding and the structures we put in place. This put us in the top rung of international best practice.

*Respecting native languages, helping and safeguarding young people, and inspiring teaching and learning are fundamental values for school leaders in an international setting. My own values are also influenced by a vibrant Christian faith which means a great deal to me, but you do not need to share my faith to stand with me on the importance of these values.*

*Leaders must believe strongly in empowering young people, placing them at the heart of all decisions. School leaders should also stand firmly behind the importance of teaching and learning. Leaders' values should include being open, transparent, honest, and caring no matter what the situation.* I'm sure there are times I don't live up to these values and vision, but they nonetheless remain as my guidance and support.

*It is when people do not connect to such values that things really start to go wrong. Without valuing learning and young people, for example, governors and staff can put other things first and get caught up in fighting the wrong battles. When you do not take time to clarify the values that will serve your life and role, your feelings can take over. This can lead you in all sorts of directions, as facts and fantasy can simply merge.*

I have experienced great things in terms of leadership everywhere I have worked, but it has not all been plain sailing! My values have helped me to navigate forward even when the waters are choppy. For me, my faith has always been a bedrock of support as times and events have unfurled around me.

Education is about so more than academic achievement; it's also about developing the whole person. Universities are crying out for young people who are critical and independent thinkers who not only know things, but know how to adapt and use them. These thinking skills give young people the ability to innovate and develop ideas, which can bring about change and help develop and improve our world.

## Student leadership

Leadership was a key focus for my work at Hallsworth, as I pulled together all the threads, I had used in the past to create strong leadership courses across the whole school. These leadership skills are something which must be taught from an early age, as we encourage young people to think for themselves, research, innovate and discover new ideas, and work as a team to support others. We need young people to serve as leaders who can develop ideas. Having students as "learning ambassadors" or "eco ambassadors," for example, can enable students to apply their learning in the community. I often held sessions with these learning ambassadors to discuss which teachings the students found most helpful, and I would feed this information back to staff.

We also developed a primary school leadership award and one for middle school, along with training in leadership and management with accredited courses as the students grew older. The International Leadership Award or Duke of Edinburgh's Award also offered bronze, silver, and gold awards. These awards encouraged self-confidence and service to others, and students who achieved them often spoke highly of them.

Of course, things didn't always run so smoothly!

One group of Kazakh students were on their expedition—a key part of the award.

"But what's wrong with our drivers taking our rucksacks in the car so we don't have to carry them?" several asked as they organised drivers to take their things and help set up their tents. They were used to things being done for them, and it was a real eye-opener that they must do things for themselves...The award helped them focus on the fact that leadership needed their hard work and input—rather than letting them sit on the side lines and get people to do things for them.

The leadership courses we introduced covered a wide range of areas to develop individual skills and interests. The essence of most of the awards was the following:

- Complete a residential experience while at the school.
- Undertake a research project involving independent learning.
- Produce the best academic results you can.
- Take part in activities with others outside of school time.
- Develop your understanding of Kazakh culture.
- Undertake some service to others.

We encouraged older students to take university online courses and formal management awards with the UK Institute of Chartered Management or another externally-validated leadership award; there were many out there. The IB Diploma programme also encouraged this approach as students entered their last two years with us.

We were aiming to launch a Hallsworth Leadership Award for older students, which would include many activities in addition to academic study, and would form the basis of an American high school diploma. By the time I left the school, we were well on the way to achieving full accreditation with the New England Association of Schools and Colleges (NEASC) and the Council of International Schools (CIC) to make this a reality. This was an incredibly important piece of work.

As I have shared, Jackie and I had a strong affinity with the local people, through our faith community and a local family, so I was delighted to help the British embassy set up a project to support young Kazakh girls in the south of the country who were often readily forced into arranged marriages. We devised a leadership scheme to encourage them to have a voice and grow in confidence. We also sent staff down to the south to work with the young girls and staff, and we won funding from the UK government for this important work. We also hosted a major international conference for the British embassy in Astana.

The scheme for the young Kazakh girls involved citizenship, teamwork, and creativity and development. The citizenship project could involve raising money for charity, running a project to benefit your local community or peer mentoring to help others. The teamwork elements could involve sports or the arts or joining a debating team. Creativity and development could involve a science project, planning new buildings for the new capital, Astana, or some kind of work experience. The girls would then have to record the hours of work they had done and reflect on and evaluate what they had achieved.

There was considerable flexibility on the projects undertaken, as different schools had differing facilities. The award had to be possible and achievable while raising confidence and leadership skills.

"When do we finally get to meet the Kazakh teachers, we are working with?" was the chorus from several of our UK staff.

A sense of excitement was building, and planning sessions laid out exactly what these staff were going to do. The plan was for them to train local teachers with a special leadership award to roll out to their young girls. I wanted students at Hallsworth to eventually get involved with the process, so we would develop not only leadership skills in these young girls, but also a growing sense of self-confidence among all our young people to make their own decisions.

*This kind of service to others is something all young people should be trained in, so they grow up seeing the needs and concerns of others as well as themselves, and so they can become caring and supportive members of society.*

Our teachers held a number of exciting sessions to train staff to deliver this Kazakh leadership award, and I was sorry to leave the country just as this key work was starting.

## The challenge of governors

Amidst these incredible experiences, challenges arose. I was aware that some governors had not fully supported my appointment, and issues soon arose. Disagreements emerged regarding my decision to limit the number of exams for students at the age of sixteen, in line with top UK university advice, and in spite of the fixed term contracts that were offered, there were inappropriate discussions about compensating staff who left under questionable circumstances or weren't aligning with the school's future direction.

Despite these obstacles, my priority remained on the students and ensuring excellent teaching for which I had strong support from the Kazakh governors. However, some UK governors continued to question my decisions. The school curriculum needed adjustments to provide more English and exam class lessons and targeted support for second language learners. I introduced a grading system aligned with a management information system, allowing us to closely monitor and support underachieving students. Rigorous attendance measures were also implemented. The school curriculum had been structured like a UK all-ability school in the 1990s, with little concession made to second language learners.

As a leader, my own performance management became centred around staff gossip rather than a thorough analysis of my accomplishments at the school. Looking back, I wondered if I did enough to bring the governors on board and ensure their understanding of our senior team's vision. While I provided written summaries for meetings, nothing compares to the value of face-to-face communication.

I had received a fair warning ahead of my appointment that the governors at Hallsworth could be challenging to work with, but I should have paid closer attention to the underlying message. Many of the governors had not realised they needed to encourage the school to move educationally with the times and changing their mindset required a great deal of patience and effort. However, I firmly believe that any time spent with governors is never wasted. If I had invested more time in building relationships with them, seeking their opinions, and rallying them to support my vision, I may have garnered more backing when it mattered most. Although working in an international school with UK-based governors presented its challenges, I could have found ways to bridge the gap. *Hindsight is a wonderful thing! My leadership advice is to tread carefully and invest as much time as you possibly can with governors, helping them share your vision. This won't necessarily avoid problems, but it could pay you dividends when you least expect it.*

Despite the challenges, I enjoyed my time in Astana enormously. So did my wife, Jackie, who ran very popular cooking classes for younger pupils and enjoyed talking with parents and staff alike.

"Where is Mrs Ullmer?" I heard many young children ask as they excitedly looked forward to their weekly cooking lessons. We had to ration student involvement, as the lessons became so popular that we couldn't fit everyone in. Soon, Kazakh delicacies and English chocolate brownies emerged, with ever-smiling faces behind them!

## Saying farewell...

So where does this story of leadership and incredible experiences lead to? *Knowing when to stand down and defer to others is a key aspect of leadership. We are always training the leaders of tomorrow, and one day we must hand the responsibility over to them.*

For me, health and difficult circumstances provided the cue for retirement, but all kinds of factors can lead to it. *Getting your work-life balance is crucial at any stage of life, but particularly so when it comes to times to retire.* I had been extremely ill, having worked almost non-stop to rectify the problems I had discovered at the school. Evenings often finished late, with me writing policies to share with staff and resolving issues on structure and process which had not been dealt with previously.

"Jonathan, your mother is taking a turn for the worse," I was told in an urgent call from England. My mother was in her nineties and living in a home, which was nearly next door to us so Jackie and I could easily visit and send friends to see her as well. She loved taking rides in a mobility scooter with Jackie and seeing everything that was going on. Earlier that term, we had decided that Jackie would return to the UK to be on hand to support my mother as we were concerned about her steady deterioration. As news got worse, I swiftly returned to see her and we had an amazing time. We spent time together sharing stories, and I updated her on latest amusing tales from Kazakhstan, including the horror Philippa had experienced when she tasted horse milk there for the first time. It was extraordinarily healthy, but I just couldn't persuade her to believe me. My mother had been a teacher early in her career and was always so supportive of everything her children did over the years. She had seen my sisters work in Kenya and Pakistan, and always had a heart for work overseas.

It's very hard to take on board when an end is coming, but I returned to Astana as the school inspection was upon us. It was immediately after the inspection that I had a call from Jackie.

"Jonathan, darling, the doctors are going to withdraw treatment, and it's not looking good."

The next morning, I got the news that my mother had passed away, which was hard to accept or understand. I was hurting so very much inside, and felt overwhelmed as I struggled to appear normal and support the staff. *However, sometimes you have to hold your own feelings in check as a leader, and remember we are here to serve and that others have needs too.* After a long and difficult time at inspection, the staff needed good news and congratulating, and it was important to go into school to share the great inspection results with them. They all had a wonderful time and I was grateful for the positive results amidst my pain.

Meanwhile my wife continued to have serious concerns about my own health and we sought a second opinion on what the local doctors were saying about my condition. We approached Dr Ruth Bush, a professor of medicine and surgery in the United States. After investigating my condition, she wrote clearly and bluntly that if left untreated, it would "rapidly become life-threatening." It was time to act. If I continued as I had been, I had been clearly warned of the consequences, and I certainly didn't feel that I was at all ready to meet my maker!

With hindsight, thirty years of working in difficult schools had taken their toll. During the final inspection which I had just completed at Hallsworth, I was confined to a wheelchair at times. A doctor came in at regular intervals to give me pain-killing injections, much to the consternation of my Kazakh staff and senior leadership who were aware of it. I knew this was no way to live, and I felt the concerns of many around me. Kazakh staff kindly arranged a rota to be in my apartment while I was asleep and ill as they were so concerned about me.

Another unexpected issue came up at the same time as my health problems and death of my mother. One issue that teachers are very vulnerable to at any time in their career are accusations of abuse, particularly with the flourishing of the "me-too" movement. This awareness is generally a good thing that can provide relief from genuine abuse, but sadly it also can facilitate others in making false accusations. Unfortunately, I finally experienced it myself at the end of my career when quite unexpectedly, a sixth form student from twenty-five years ago before made some false accusations against me which I can only assume were to further his journalistic and speaking career. Much of his work I had seen up till then had consisted of attacking people in print who he had worked with or been associated with for financial remuneration, so I certainly wasn't alone in being ruthlessly targeted in the press and beyond. It turned out later that he was having some marital issues and also made a string of allegations about his father who had just died which also fitted in with this pattern. But it was still a devastating and really sad experience which left me reeling. *As a leader in the twenty-first century, we have to be so aware of these issues and the potential dangers all around us. For many years as a headteacher I had warned staff about the risks we all face, never dreaming I would be the person who would have to stand up against them. Accusations are so easy to make and in the hands of manipulative people can be highly dangerous. When these situations arise its wise, amongst other actions, to direct allegations straight to the police so baseless claims like these ones can be investigated and dismissed.*

However, before I knew what was happening, governors without experience of these issues chose to use the false allegations they had been told about me as an opportunity to try and force me to leave. I was told they had already met behind closed doors and then called me to a meeting just before my mother's funeral. I didn't know the content of the meeting in advance or have the chance to take legal advice. With so much going on with my own health and dealing with the loss of a much-loved parent, along with unpleasant attacks, I just didn't have the heart to fight. It was made clear to me that all the governors had already made up their minds, and once you lose the support of your governors, there is little point fighting it. To try to preserve the reputation of the school I had worked so hard for, and as I was told decisions had been made without my input, I agreed to resign on health grounds.

I had always spoken warmly of Hallsworth as their head teacher, telling students in assemblies about their sense of fair play and strong values. This experience left me greatly saddened afterwards to feel this didn't always appear to be true.

A friend later reminded me it had always been my intention to retire just before I was sixty. I had completely forgotten, and she was quite right. Years of working in difficult schools had taken their physical toll, and it was time to step back. This was a wise and logical step to take, and I realised I probably needed a jolt to do it. When you come to retire, you have to lay down all your successes and achievements, frustrations and missed opportunities. It is time for someone else to take up the baton and you have to accept this. I was always impressed by Queen Elizabeth when she was asked what she was most looking forward to in the next life. She replied that she looked forward to laying her crown at the feet of Jesus. This laying down of responsibility comes for many of us when we retire, and I have spoken earlier of the importance of having your core beliefs and knowing who you are. You must work hard not to be defined by your job and what happens to you, as there is so much more in life. If you have that solid core of beliefs and a sense of what defines you, then you can step aside and leave your roles to others, content in who you are and what you have achieved.

Meanwhile, the results of the inspection at Hallsworth School Astana in November 2018 put us among the top international best practices in seventeen of nineteen areas, including pastoral care and safeguarding. The report spoke of "a culture of positive behaviour" with a "supportive approach to feedback." It further recorded, "Student achievement is celebrated in various forums with appropriate and student-friendly systems for praise and rewards. The removal of the negative 'points' system and a more child-centred system for sanctions has been a positive step. Students spoke keenly about this in their interviews, and upper school students were exceptionally happy about the focus on positive reinforcement of habits." Our team had enjoyed setting these new systems in place, and it was great to see these changes celebrated with us. The Kazakh department was spoken of as being "highly successful" with lessons of "excellent quality." The report also spoke warmly of the "mutual respect between the students and teachers." With regard to leadership, the report spoke of their "high expectations to drive improvement" with academic progress "a high priority." The school's leadership was described as expressing a "clarity of vision with confidence and…a willingness to engage in improvements it has highlighted." After all the hard work behind the scenes to support governance, the warm approval was welcomed.

We had set the school up to offer American high school diplomas, with new grading systems ready to go, while rebuilding the curriculum and transforming their safeguarding practice to outstanding levels. That—along with being able to lead an amazing team and being graded "excellent" in all areas at Chatsdean School, including pastoral care and academic success—speaks for itself. I was particularly proud of the team who had worked so hard with me to be named the Boarding School of the Year. I had already in 2017 had an amazing send off from Chatsdean School when the school hired Leeds Castle in Kent for the night with guests of honour from local schools and the Independent Schools Association in the UK. It was a moving occasion full of fun and laughter which I still remember today.

I had achieved all that I had set out to do, and the world of retirement beckoned.

Teaching young people and working with schools became an amazing career, and I felt incredibly privileged to have worked with so many outstanding people. Empowering young people and helping them speak out was always at the heart of my vision—resolutely supporting the importance of teaching and learning while working to make it as great as it can be. I hoped I had also helped others in their own leadership paths into the future, as one of the key tasks of leadership is preparing for those who go after you.

*When you have a vision, you need to stick to it and stand by it. Integrity, honesty, and transparency should be your watchwords. No matter what happens, if you are guided by these values, you are unlikely to go far wrong. Hold your head high, do your best, and keep smiling. You may meet with incredible difficulties on the way, and as a leader anything can be thrown at you. But remember that you can help shape thousands of lives over your career; what higher calling can there be than that?*

## Good leadership when problems arise

- **Watch carefully when things are not as they are said to be**. It's easy for schools or governors to delude themselves as to what's going on. Great buildings and money alone do not make a good school. Ensuring success is a lot harder work than this. Look beyond what you are told. Then move quickly to see the real picture, so you can do

176

something about it.

- **Always seek second opinions**. You often need extra help and leadership capacity to do what needs to be done. Find independent experts to come in and test what you find, providing support and advice to supplement your own. Be reflective and analytical and make sure you back up what you find, so you are certain about what you are dealing with.

- **Be unfazed by things that go wrong**. Whatever you do, things will go wrong at times. You then just need to regroup, back off, or move forward—whatever is appropriate. Stay calm and cool in the midst of crisis, and think hard about options before committing yourself.

- **Stand by values and vision**. While doing this, you of course must be constantly re-examining and challenging what you believe in. Some values like transparency, honesty, and decency are universal for good leaders; others are values you develop for yourself. All are important and need refreshing regularly.

- **Know when to walk away**. All of us as leaders should be preparing for those who will replace us in our roles. We owe it to our profession to develop leaders of the future, and one day they will take our place. Knowing when that day has come is not always easy. It can be forced upon you, it may happen by design and planning, but that day will certainly come. If you know you have lost the support of your governors, then you are unlikely to win and need to go with good grace.

# Chapter 8
# Courageous Leadership

*Let people fly…*

There is no such thing as a "super head" or infallible CEO. This chapter is about summarising and exploring further some of the key leadership lessons we have touched on in the book, and showing how to lead a school to outstanding results.

Great institutions do not depend on top-down management from on high. They are managed and led at all levels. Powerful middle management must be created to drive ideas, so they can impact throughout the school.

As you can see, there is certainly a clear overlap between schools and corporations; much of what I have said can be readily adapted to leading a wide range of institutions. My own specialism has been in educational leadership, but the lessons extend far beyond this.

When you first start at a difficult school and when things are tough, a more directive approach is often important, but this is only a stage to go though. It's never somewhere to stay.

## Training

Training is essential and it must be a high priority in terms of spending. Many schools or companies see it as the first thing to cut, when it often needs to be the last. Whole-school training, closely aligned to vision and mission, is effective but only part of the picture. Middle leaders must be trained effectively. (I always tried to get mine to train with University College London.) You need excellent and effective training which really puts people through their paces and shows them how to manage others and get results.

## Coaching

A coaching system is essential to helping staff support each other in a non-threatening way. New ideas and approaches should be encouraged and tested as a collaborative culture is encouraged. Coaching helps create an enthused and determined workforce who will really bring results.

Your coaches need strong and effective training so they can reflect and encourage great ideas. With staff fully on board and encouraging each other, things really start to flourish.

This coaching must of course be completely separate from any disciplinary system. And it does not need to be done by your immediate manager or head of department; in fact, it's far better if it isn't. Department management structures can pick up underperformance and set targets for improvement, but a coaching system is something completely different.

We did some great work with "triads"—groups of three teachers who were given time off during several weeks in the term to meet and discuss an aspect of teaching they wanted to improve. They held each other to account and kept a record of what they were doing and the outcomes. This practice is a great way for staff to take ownership of their training, and a mark of a successful school with confident staff.

## Selecting staff and structures

When you are in the early stages of improvement, of course, you first must identify great middle managers. Then be quite directive until people are ready and trained to take over key roles themselves.

Staff changes may also need to be made for those who really aren't up to it, and you must go through the process to dismiss poor performing staff on grounds of capability. Another option is of course a re-structure, in which you streamline processes and remove staff roles which are no longer needed. This needs to be handled with fairness and transparency, as everyone must be given the opportunity to change. My experience at Oxford showed just how some staff were really enthusiastic about change, and it showed it's not only possible but really great when it happens.

With strong middle managers in place, you also need to identify your coaches—those who are really good at their jobs and can support others. This allows more people to be involved in the vision and mission of the school or company and will support middle managers by driving excellence.

## Values, vision and reflection

It's also vital, as I have raised earlier, to have clear values and a mission behind your operations and actions. This will sustain and support you during the darker days you may have to face.

For me, faith in a loving and encompassing God has been my watchword—a God who is personal and real and who challenges and supports. He won't stop me from facing the darkness, but he will stand with me as I face it.

You may of course walk a different path, but there must be something at the core of your being that sustains and strengthens you. I would challenge you to discover what this can be. You may then go on your own voyage as I have. Don't be so caught up in the day-to-day rush of life that you lack the time to sit back and consider what it all means.

The best leaders are those who can serve others. They are self-reflective and look at how they can change themselves, rather than seeing fault in others. The hallmark of a good leader is one who enables others to be coached and supported. A good leader listens and is able to serve others. This is the model Jesus gave us as the servant king, and it is those who put service to others—first, at all levels—who really become great leaders.

## Policies and performance management

There are many practical things you can do to support your leadership—such as checking over your policies and making sure they are accurate and owned by people. You must be realistic in that staff are unlikely to read them, though you can get them to take an online safeguarding course, regularly covering key areas ranging from female genital mutilation to basic safeguarding. There are some excellent courses out there which cover most of the really key areas, and this guarantees that staff have engaged with these topics at some level. Your training days can then focus on other policy areas, ensuring they have been engaged with and discussed.

Performance management can be done online as well. Systems like "Blue Sky" and others can help to guarantee that there has been genuine engagement and agreement, as all areas must be signed off by both parties. This also ensures your vision and values are embedded in regular performance management.

## Leadership at all levels

As you can see from this book, my own focus has been very much on leadership at all levels. It's not just about being a great leader yourself, but it also involves encouraging these leadership skills in others, including students and staff alike. Setting up leadership awards with young people fosters independent learning, involving some level of independent research while providing challenges that encouraged young people to think. Following, for example, is the award for eleven- to fourteen-year-olds I designed at Hallsworth Astana. It sums up the philosophy behind much of the leadership awards I was involved in launching with students.

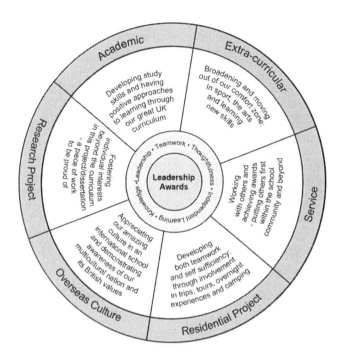

The leadership award covers academic skills, involvement in extracurricular activities, service, residential project, local culture, and research. You can quite easily set the levels that students need to attain in each area. We also had awards in other year groups, with a university-style approach for the Hallsworth Diploma for sixteen- to eighteen-year-olds in the sixth form.

"Mr Jonathan, I've just become an eco-ambassador," one student told me as she rushed down the corridor. "I want to know how much energy the school uses and how we can reduce it."

This was great to hear! I led them over to the bursar to explore some of the issues and what to do about them.

For older students, we created opportunities for students to be involved as university ambassadors, school council members, communications ambassadors, and sports ambassadors as we looked for a wide range of areas of service for young people to be involved in. There were academic achievements students could complete with FutureLearn.com, where they could take university courses which interested them, often certificated by top universities. There were also summer programmes and internships. We worked out a special diploma, like the one I spoke of earlier at Chatsdean School, with achievements in key areas which would be of interest to universities. They covered service, academics, and a range of other areas and were advertised in a glossy booklet. You can also incorporate an extended essay Advanced-level qualification.

What we then worked out was by combining these with previous success at GCSE and IB or Advanced-level subjects studied, we had the basis of an American high school diploma. This was a step further than what I had done in Canterbury. It was exciting stuff, and we were not slow to achieve CIS and NEASC accreditation from the States.

Leadership was a focus I particularly wanted to focus on to give purpose and meaning to the lives of students, but you may have your own ideas which match what you want to achieve. The ideas I have shared helped to created excellence in the schools I worked in, with the best example being the comprehensive, whole-school setup I created with staff at Hallsworth Astana.

I have certainly made my own mistakes along the way, as you will too. But perseverance certainly pays off.

Young people must be stretched and challenged, and the leadership awards provide that stretch for gifted and talented young people, while also being inclusive and open to all to partake in. Leadership is not something for the few; it's something everybody should be trained in. The skills needed are vital ones for life.

## Be courageous

As I have shown at the end of each chapter, developing leadership skills is about becoming a better person—listening to others, supporting and training, challenging and achieving objectives. If you master many of these skills, you will find more focus and direction not only in your job, but also in life. You will not necessarily get an easy ride, no matter how prepared you are, but always remember that there is light shining somewhere in the darkness which will help you through.

You will need courage for those difficult meetings with parents or governors which may be unfair, ill-informed, and potentially dangerous. Courage is not something you just "have"—it can be a learned skill. Prepare yourself well and walk forward with confidence, and courage will soon find you. There will be times you fall flat on your face, but it takes courage to pick yourself up and keep going as if nothing has happened. Learn from your mistakes, then go out with renewed vigour—keeping your vision and values firmly in front of you.

## Four key stages of leadership

There are four key stages of leadership I have tried to articulate. They don't necessarily come in this order, as every school and situation are different, but this does give some pointers as to how things may develop.

**Stage One**

When in a school requiring urgent improvement, a more directive approach may be relevant. You may just need to say what has to be done and ensure it's completed. This is hard work and revolves a lot around you. Managing this yourself is okay for a short period, but clearly it isn't sustainable. Whole-staff training is vital here; you must set clear parameters and expectations for the whole school.

I enjoyed running sessions on what staff felt a great school was, and then moving on with their ideas. When you do this, you need to celebrate good practices from the start and listen carefully to staff concerns.

Hard decisions may need to be made on staff and structures to ensure they are all fit for purpose. You also need to start to develop leadership skills in key parts of the student body.

**Stage Two**

Once your baselines and expectations are clear at all levels, identify those who are skilled practitioners and ensure they are mentored and supported. Those who are weaker need targeted help to improve—such as a mentor who works alongside staff to help them with ideas and producing great lessons.

Your school needs to move forward at all levels, and training should be targeted carefully with staff involvement. Ask staff which areas they think they need help with, and use lesson observation evidence to check what you need to focus on throughout the school.

Work hard to develop a supportive culture where expectations are high, but staff are supported and supported in attaining them. Regular meetings between senior staff and people they manage helps to cascade ideas while ensuring they are being implemented. Instead of just the head pushing directives, they become far more of a group effort.

You must encourage staff to reflect on their work and look for ways to support students further. Independent learning should be encouraged throughout the curriculum, as staff and students alike are encouraged to be self-reflective and independent learners.

**Stage Three**

Continue to develop staff, so they are involved in leading the training of others. Mentorship is expanded, with new mentors trained and appointed who are able to lead in these areas and encourage staff to keep improving. You need to grow new leaders from within and help new teachers develop confidence and enthusiasm with the profession.

My staff in Canterbury set up "Leadmeets," where leaders could share ideas, as well as "Teachmeets," where teachers came and spoke for ten minutes on a particular technique, they had used in the classroom which was successful for them. We all learned so much from this.

**Stage Four**

This is crucial. Staff should be encouraged to fly—leading their own training, undertaking teaching research, and mentoring and supporting others, with clear pathways for staff as they develop their skills. You also should be training up your successors and those who will go into leadership positions—with the right skills, ready to benefit the rest of the profession.

Self-reflection is crucial, as is encouraging it in others. When things go wrong, look at ways *you* could have handled it better, rather than how *they* could have handled it better.

This is the ideal stage to be in, as staff are involved in leadership and improvement, and their ideas can have real impact. University links allow validation of work achieved, and for new staff it feels a lively and vibrant place to be a part of.

## And to end it all...

*Being a great leader involves, in many ways, "jumping out of the window." You must leave your safe space and have a clear focus on the skills outlined in this book.*

*You can develop these skills not only for yourself but for students and others too. Empowering those around you to take the initiative, challenge, and hold others to account will move your school forward. It will also bring many great satisfactions as they are helped to move forward with new skills and support.*

*Leadership is not for the few; it is for everyone. Students from primary age upwards can be given the chance to develop independent thinking and leadership skills, including more formal qualifications for senior students. Staff also need strong training opportunities to develop leadership skills in a fast-moving and exciting educational landscape.*

*A great school develops the approaches within this book at all levels and for everyone. It's not hard to do, but you need a clear structure and awards that motivate and develop core leadership skills, which you will find is an incredible motivator for staff and students alike.*

*The days of ineffectual school councils and irrelevant training days should be well and truly over. Staff and students need to be empowered with genuine ownership in their schools to create great, forward-thinking institutions.*

*There will always be naysayers or those who try and find fulfilment by tearing down others; just leave them behind and focus on what really matters. Negativity and unpleasantness never bring fulfilment and success.*

I have been amazed by my career in teaching. I have loved every part of it, including: encouraging students to develop in school productions when they enthusiastically worked all hours because they were trusted and treated as adults, and serving as a head teacher when I was able to develop leadership courses and opportunities across the whole school.

You need to carry your team behind you, with students also on board through activities that stretch and challenge them. And then you will be well on the way to creating an excellent school. Go for it!

Further information and support can be found at: *www.excellenceineducation.com*